Communities in Britain

The CHINESE in BRITAIN

Anthony Shang

Batsford Academic and Educational
London

Contents

Typeset by Tek-Art Ltd, Kent
and printed in Spain by
Grijelmo SA, Bilbao
for the publishers
Batsford Academic and Educational,
an imprint of B.T. Batsford Ltd,
4 Fitzhardinge Street
London W1H 0AH

ISBN 0 7134 4236 0

To my father, Richard Shang Yu Sheng, who in his lifetime never ceased to remind me of my cultural heritage.

Acknowledgments

This book was written very much as a cooperative venture. Without the patience, consideration, advice and help of the Wan, Chow and Chan families, specifically David Wan, Shing Tung Chow and Alfred Chan, it would not have been possible to write the book in its present form. The author would also like to thank all those in the Chinese community who lent their time and kind assistance during the research stage. Special thanks also to Guida Crowley who so willingly at short notice typed parts of the manuscript.

Introduction

The Chinese today form the third largest visible minority group in Britain. Yet little is known about the Chinese, where they came from, why they came here, what they are doing in Britain, their cultural beliefs and aspirations. Existing literature on this subject is either sparse, out-of-date or caters to a more specialized readership.

Because information about the Chinese in Britain is not widely available, existing stereotypes govern our notions of them. These stereotypes are based on the alien nature of Chinese names, different physical features and commonly associated occupations of Chinese immigrants. It is true that most Chinese in Britain are in the catering business. Yet the Chinese community is a very diverse one, not only in the occupational sense but also in the geographical origins of its members.

To provide a personal dimension to the community's history, experience, beliefs and aspirations, three Chinese families, the Wans, Chows and Chans, have been selected to relate their stories and express their deep-felt views. Although typical in some respects, the families chosen are in no way totally representative of all the Chinese in Britain. The Wans are from a village in the New Territories, Hong Kong and currently run a take-away in Bethnal Green. By contrast, the Chow family originally came from Shandong province in North East China. The Chows own two Chinese restaurants in Tring, Hertfordshire, and Enfield in Middlesex. The Chans, Alfred and Alice, have an urban background, coming from the town of Tsuen Wan in Hong Kong. Unlike the Wans and the Chows, most of their family are still in Hong Kong.

In attempting to provide a broad overview of the Chinese community, generalizations and simplification of sometimes complex events and issues are necessary. In no way, therefore, does the author claim this work to be totally representative or typical of the experiences of all the Chinese in Britain. Having said this, this study should provide the reader with a useful introduction to the history and way of life of one of Britain's least-known minority communities.

The author in his North London flat.

Who are the Chinese?

The span of recorded Chinese history covers 3,500 years, dating back to the Shang Dynasty in 1520 BC. Large-scale migration from China, by comparison, is fairly recent and confined to the last 150 years.

Until recently, the origins of Chinese culture were said to be rooted in mythological kings, who passed on the skills of farming, fishing, silkworm breeding and silk weaving to the indigenous population. Whilst scholars offer differing opinions on the origin of the Chinese, archaeological discoveries of fossil remains, in the last 60 years, suggest that the Chinese originated no more than a day's journey away from the modern capital Peking. More recent excavations, at different sites, lend weight to the possibility that a culture which could be called "Chinese" existed not only in the Yellow River Basin, the historic heartland of China, but also in a number of regions which are part of modern China today.

Chinese civilization has not suffered the same fate as the other great agricultural civilizations of ancient times, such as the Maya in Central America, and the civilizations of Mesopotamia and Egypt. China's cultural heritage has been both preserved and maintained, right up to the present day. It is documented in historical records, embodied in works of art such as paintings, calligraphy and carvings, and expressed in the form of literature and daily customs.

The Overseas Chinese

Chinese migration represents an important part of the history of human migration. Certainly, the movement of people out of China contributed to the growth of multi-racial societies in South East Asia, the South Pacific, North and South America, Europe and Africa.

Large-scale migration to Britain and Western Europe is quite recent, compared with the number of Chinese who left for the Americas, Australia and South East Asia as coolies and contract labourers in the nineteenth century. The Chinese who came to Britain after the Second World War differ in one significant respect from their nineteenth-century predecessors. Many of the Chinese who live in Britain today came from Hong Kong – including the families Wan, Chow and Chan, whose biographies and experience form part of this book. By contrast, perhaps as many as 90 per cent of those recruited as coolies or contract labourers in the last century originated from the southern Chinese provinces of Guangdong and Fujian.

The remainder of this chapter gives a historical review of the growth of Chinese settlements overseas. Undoubtedly, the Chinatown communities of San Francisco, Vancouver and Ho Chi Minh City (Vietnam) owe their origins to the earlier phase of migration. The Chinese in Britain are the most recent overseas Chinese community to carve out a niche for itself in a foreign land.

There are estimated to be over 25 million Chinese living overseas today. This does not include the 22 million inhabitants of Taiwan and the territory of Hong Kong, who are referred to by the Communist Government of mainland China as *tong bao* (compatriots) and not just *hua qiao* (overseas Chinese). The largest settlements are in South East Asia, or *Nanyang*, as it is known to the Chinese migrants. Broadly speaking, migration took place in three waves.

The first wave took place during the Tang

A Straits-born Chinese lady crossing the road in Singapore. Many of the Straits-born Chinese in Singapore and Malaysia are integrated into the culture of the indigenous society.

Dynasty (618-906 AD), with the establishment of seasonal agricultural movement between the mainland and Formosa (Taiwan) and Pescadores. Chinese traders also began to follow the coastal routes to South East Asia during this period. In fact, one of the earliest references to Chinese communities overseas comes from a thirteenth-century Mongolian emissary to Cambodia. These Chinese settlers were referred to as "men of the Sea", which suggests that they were coastal traders or pirates.

During the Ming Dynasty (1368-1644), Chinese explorers and traders ventured as far as Africa and Madagascar. Already by this time, Chinese traders were following the trade routes of the Arabs to Malacca (in Malaysia today), the East Indies (present-day Indonesia) and the Philippines. In 1712 the northern Manchu rulers of China, who wanted to prevent the departure of "sympathizers" of the previous Ming Dynasty, issued an Imperial Edict prohibiting the return of overseas Chinese (and thus, in fact, banishing them). By this time, however, there were well-established Chinese communities

Chinese labourers at work building the Central Pacific Railroad.

living in what is known as Vietnam and Thailand today. By 1880, over one quarter of Siam's (Thailand) population of 6 million were ethnic Chinese.

The third wave, which began in the 1840s, represented a new epoch in migration, as millions of Chinese left their native towns and villages in southern China to work on plantations and in mines in Spanish America, Indonesia, Malaysia, North America and Australia. After the abolition of the slave trade, a demand for labour in British, Spanish and Dutch colonies was the main force behind the recruitment of Chinese "coolies" to the West Indies and Latin America. Other "free" migrants went to the USA, Australia and other places, as contract labourers and gold prospectors.

Many factors led to the outflow of able-bodied males from their native villages. Increased taxation levied on the peasants by the Manchu rulers, to pay off their foreign debts, had become an intolerable burden by the late nineteenth century. Frequent crop failures and natural disasters made it difficult enough for the large population to eke out a living. Finally, the Taiping Rebellion, which started in the province of Guangxi in 1851, caused severe dislocations to the agrarian economy and devastated vast tracts of land. The rebels, fighting under the banner of "Heavenly Kingdom of Great Peace", had egalitarian aims and were opposed to the oppressive rule of the late Manchu Emperors.

What was characteristic of all these migrants was their dream of returning home to their native land one day, with wealth and newly acquired status. They, therefore, saw themselves as "sojourners", rather than immigrants to a foreign country. However, by 1930, more than 8 million Chinese had settled throughout the world. Despite the horrors of the "coolie" trade, which involved the massacre of hundreds of Chinese in Mexico, by 1950, more than 60,000 Chinese had settled in Latin America. Even the small Pacific islands of Fiji, Samoa and Tahiti had sizeable Chinese populations by this time. This pattern of settlement was more a result of the early "sojourners" failing to accumulate the necessary wealth to return home, rather than of any conscious desire to assimilate into a new society.

A key aspect of overseas Chinese communities at this time was the importance of kinship ties, based on blood, marriage and sometimes adoption. This was largely due to the demographic organization of their native villages in South China, which often were inhabited by one clan or a single lineage of the clan. However, kinship loyalties were, partially, overridden by ties of dialect and district, as it was common for migrants from villages in a particular district or dialect-area to migrate to the same place. Most of the ethnic Chinese in Vietnam were, therefore, originally from Hainan Island and Guangdong province. Those in the Philippines were from the district of Amoy in Fujian province.

During the early days of British colonial rule, Hong Kong acted as a transhipment point for Chinese "coolies" to the West Indies, Spanish America and the Indian Ocean islands. Plantation owners contracted British merchants to procure "coolies". They, in turn, hired Chinese "brokers" (labour contractors) to recruit "coolies". Most of those recruited were prisoners captured in clan fights, victims of kidnapping, and persons with gambling debts. The "coolie" trade was as cruel as the earlier slave trade. The mortality rate was high on the packed ships. In 1855, the British government passed the Chinese Passengers' Act which banned the transportation of "coolies" from Hong Kong on British flagships. However, this only served to drive the trade to the neighbouring Portuguese colony of Macao.

From Rice to Gold: The American Experience

The history of American immigration is the story of hope, ambition and cruel disappointments for most newcomers to California, then known as "Gold Mountain" to the thousands of peasants of Guangdong province who had embarked on the voyage to discover gold.

Labour shortages, particularly in California, caused by the preoccupation of white settlers with gold prospecting, led to large-scale recruitment of labourers from China. The Chinese arrived in America not as "coolies" but as contract labourers, under the "credit ticket" system. This system was more akin to debt-bondage than a service contract. Chinese labourers were brought to the USA by six merchant *hongs* (houses) in San Francisco. The migrants were obligated to the *hongs* which advanced the ticket money and found them jobs. None could return to China until they had repaid their debts, which were compounded with high interest rates.

The 1870s was the greatest decade of immigration to the USA, with 123,201 Chinese arriving during this period. Most of the Chinese came from several districts in Guangdong province. The early migrants were largely from Sze Yap (Four Districts) or from the three "Delta" districts in Guangdong. There were also a number of *Hakka* ("Guest People") who had settled in southern China in the last 200 years. The *Hakka*, a migratory people of North East China with their own dialect, migrated southwards from the thirteenth century.

Although most of the Chinese in America lived at poverty level, they still earned more than in China. Yet, for many, the dream of striking it rich remained just that. Expecting to return home within two years, many had not imagined the hardships they would encounter, such as extortionate rents, forced labour and physical abuse against them. By 1882, pressure from white workers and settlers brought about the Chinese Exclusion Act, which severely restricted further immigration.

The history of the early Chinese immigrants is not a happy one, as they became the victims of different forms of discrimination and racist violence. In California, Chinese gold miners were confined to exhausted, unproductive mines. After the civil war in 1867, California opposed suffrage to Negroes and Chinese. The California Supreme Court also ruled that Chinese, Negroes and mulattos were not allowed to give evidence in favour of or against a white man.

Following the civil war, raids upon the Chinese occurred at regular intervals; their property was looted and their lodgings burnt and stoning and lynching of Chinese workers by white mobs continued unabated. White opposition was often couched in racist terms, which regarded Asians as inferior beings. Samuel Gomperg, leader of the American Federation of Labour, at the end of the last century, considered the "yellows" natural liars, cheaters and murderers.

By the 1870s the Chinese began entering other occupations and many moved on to other states. Many had been employed by the Central Pacific Railway on the railroads. In fact, the penetration of the Californian mountains by the railways had been possible only because of the hard work of Chinese labourers. Market gardening, seasonal farm work and domestic service later became popular occupations for the Chinese.

2

The First Chinese in Britain

Large-scale migration of Chinese to Britain and Western Europe is comparatively recent. Despite a hundred years' historical presence in Britain, up to the last war there were fewer than 5,000 Chinese living in the country. Today, reliable estimates suggest that Britain's Chinese population exceeds 150,000, forming the third largest visible minority community. The total number of Chinese living in Western Europe today is somewhere between 6-700,000, a ten-fold increase since the 1930s. Outside Britain, most of the Chinese have settled in Holland, West Germany and France.

No community, however, no matter how close-knit, is totally homogenous. In Britain, the Chinese community is fairly diverse in terms of the geographical origins of its members and the experiences of those from rural and urban backgrounds. Furthermore, the circumstances affecting the earliest arrivals were quite different from the situations in which the post-war migrants found themselves.

From Salt to Soapy Water (The First Chinatowns)

Apart from a handful of diplomats and students, the Chinese first came to Britain as seamen. The earliest account of Chinese in Britain goes back to 1851, when there were reportedly 78 mainland Chinese living in London.

Some of the earliest arrivals came from the USA, at the end of the last century. Many were fleeing American persecution, as they were driven in their thousands from their homes in California. Chinese students came to Britain as early as 1901. The author's grandfather was one of the first Chinese

scholars to obtain a higher degree from a British university. By 1931, there were 450 Chinese students in British universities. Over half of them came from mainland China, although 120 were Chinese from Malaya.

The opening up of the China trade to British and other European merchants, after China's defeat in the Opium Wars in the second half of the nineteenth century, increased the need for Chinese seamen. They were initially recruited by the British East India

The author's grandfather, Shang Shao Kan, one of the first Chinese students to study in Britain.

Chinatown, London, 1911.

Company, from a number of southern Chinese villages. In 1868 the Liverpool shippers Alfred & Philip Holt started the first direct steamship from Europe to China, and Chinese seamen were soon seen in large numbers in British ports such as Liverpool, Cardiff and London.

In London, a Chinatown began to build up from the 1880s, in the Limehouse district bordering on the West India Docks. Streets such as Limehouse Causeway and Pennyfields had Chinese grocery stores, eating houses and meeting places, or *fongs*, providing a sense of community for the local Chinese living there. The *fongs* were a safe haven where the Chinese could relax and meet. Verbal abuse was one thing; the Limehouse Chinese also had to put up with physical abuse such as having horse dung thrown at them. Chinese street names such as Ming Street, and streets named after Chinese cities –

Pekin, Nanking and Canton – suggest that the Chinese had made a visible impact in the Limehouse area.

Similarly, in Liverpool, the area taking in Pitt Street, Cleveland Square and Frederick Street became known as a Chinese district. By 1911, there were 668 China- and Hong-Kong-born Chinese in London, 502 in Liverpool and a smaller number in Cardiff. Probably as many as half were non-resident seamen; the remainder had earlier jumped ship, to find jobs on-shore. The majority of seamen came from the Sze Yap district of Guangdong province. Indeed, the inscriptions on the gravestones in the Chinese section of Anfield cemetery (Liverpool) clearly bear this out.

Those Chinese seamen who jumped ship sought better-paid work. Some jumped ship, only to register as sailors again in a British port. This then entitled them to the same rates of pay as British seamen. The early Chinatown at this time contained a few provision stores and restaurants geared to the needs of Chinese seamen, dock workers and students. However, it was the introduction of Chinese laundries which saw the Chinese move away from dockland occupations. The growth in the Chinese laundry business was quite astronomical, so that by 1931 there were 800 such laundries in Britain. Setting up such a business required little capital other than small premises and a steam iron. Running a laundry, however, meant sheer hard work for the early migrants who would wash every item of the customers' dirty clothes by hand.

The use of cheap Chinese labour on British ships was seen as a threat by British seamen. However, Chinese sailors comprised only 1,136 of the 29,028 foreign seamen on British merchant ships in 1911 (Irene Loh Lynn, *The Chinese Community in Liverpool*, 1982, p.12). The fact that the Chinese were visibly different made them easy targets of victimization. Also, the image of China at the time as "a nation of coolies" must have rubbed off on the early migrants in Britain. Chinese seamen were regarded as strike-breakers. Their preoccupation with accumulating savings as fast as possible, before returning home, meant that they saw their employment in a different light from British seamen. Hostilities came to a head in 1911, during the seamen's strike in Cardiff. British sailors, unable to stop Chinese seamen from working, turned on the Chinese laundry shops in Cardiff.

As a result of newly imposed immigration restrictions, the Chinese population in Liverpool and London declined in the two decades after 1911. The Aliens Restriction Act 1914 established an immigration department to restrict the movement of aliens during wartime. An amendment to the Act in 1919 extended these restrictions into peace-time. The restrictions made it difficult for aliens to land, unless they were able to be self-supporting. The shipping slump during the recession in the 1920s and 1930s also saw many Chinese returning to China. And slum clearance, too, forced the old Liverpool Chinatown community to disperse. The blitz during the Second World War destroyed many of the buildings in the Limehouse District. Today, post-war housing estates now line the streets in Limehouse where the Chinese once worked and lived. Chinese restaurants and take-aways, opened perhaps in the last 10-20 years, provide the only reminder of the early Chinese presence here.

A new group of Chinese arrived in Britain at the beginning of the Second World War. These were mainly migrants from Zhejiang province and Shanghai, recruited as sailors for the Chinese Merchant Seamen's Pool, which had its wartime H.Q. in Liverpool. After the war, many seamen returned to China. Those who remained found work in a new section of the economy, the restaurant trade. As we shall see, this move into catering provided the foundation for the next phase of Chinese migration into Britain. By this time, the onset of automation and the invention of the washing-machine totally destroyed the labour-intensive Chinese laundry trade.

Despite the early history of the Chinese in Britain, it was only the post-war phase of migration which established the Chinese as a permanent community here. The early seamen saw themselves as "sojourners" who, having saved enough money, would return to their home villages in southern China. Because of this lack of permanence, it took 100 years for Chinese associations to take root and proliferate in Britain.

It should be remembered that during the inter-war years, a number of Chinese found their way to Britain and to other European countries, such as Belgium, France and Germany, as students and as labourers. The Shanghai Labour Corps, for example, provided cheap manpower for unskilled labouring jobs, at a time when most of Europe's able-bodied men were conscripted to fight in the war.

The author's father (centre), Richard Shang Yu Sheng, with two cousins in their native town of Chenxi just before departing for their studies abroad (1932).

3

The Present-Day Chinese

Up to the end of the Second World War, south China had been the staging-ground for one of the largest migrations in history. However, the growth of the Chinese community in Britain is a direct result of an economic boom that took place in the 1950s and 1960s. With the growth in the Chinese restaurant trade, a much larger-scale Chinese immigration took place. This time, however, the migrants came not from mainland China but from Hong Kong, a territory acquired by Britain as a result of the Opium Wars in the nineteenth century (see Chapter Seven).

It was during this period that the Wan, Chow and Chan families came to Britain.

David Wan in his Bethnal Green flat takes a breather from his studies.

The Wan Family

David Wan is 25 years old. He came to join his parents in Britain in 1974, from his ancestral village of Cheung Lek Mei in the New Territories, Hong Kong. David's father, a farmer, came here in 1962, to work as a cook in a suburban Chinese restaurant in London. David's mother worked in London's Chinatown, as a kitchen help. Mr and Mrs Wan, who are 54 and 46 years old respectively, now own a Chinese take-away in Bethnal Green, in the East End of London. The Wans live in a pre-war council flat in Bethnal Green. Before moving to the East End in 1975, they rented a flat in Edgware, near the restaurant where Mr Wan was working. David was only 14 years old when he came to Britain, and therefore completed his secondary education in London, before enrolling for a degree course in Electrical Engineering at Thames Polytechnic. David has now graduated and is looking for work.

Besides his parents, David has an elder brother, Kenneth, in London. Kenneth arrived here a year earlier than David. Their father could not afford to fetch both sons over at the same time. As David explained, his father came to Britain "with nothing, just £5". When his parents came to Britain in 1962, David was cared for by his elder cousin in the New Territories. David's grandparents are still living in Hong Kong today. He also has a younger sister, Angela, who was born in Britain. Angela is 13 years old and is now attending comprehensive school. The Wan family gained a daughter-in-law when Kenneth married a Chinese from Liverpool in 1980. Kenneth's wife only arrived in Britain the year before. Her parents are running a take-away business in Merseyside.

11

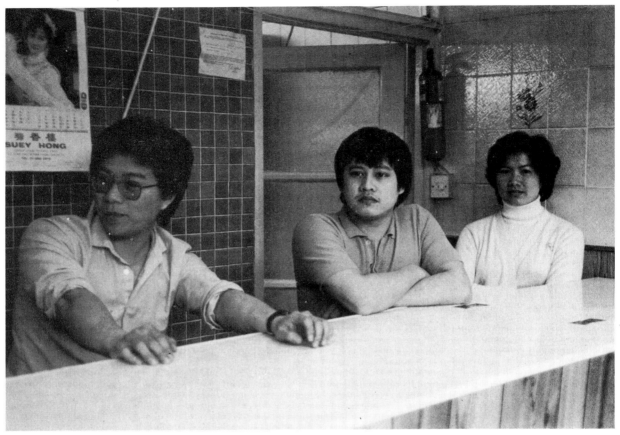

David Wan (left), his brother Kenneth and sister-in-law doing their weekend stint at the family take-away, "Suey Hong".

The Chow Family

The Chow family own two restaurants in Britain. Shing Tung Chow, 34 years old, runs the family restaurant in Tring, Hertfordshire. He came to this country from Hong Kong, to study for "O" levels, in 1967. His father arrived the year before, to join a partner in a restaurant business in Woolwich. The Chow family are not natives of Hong Kong. Shing Tung's grandparents migrated to Hong Kong from Shandong province in north China, after the Communist takeover in 1949. Although born in Hong Kong, Shing Tung spent his childhood in the northern Chinese cities of Tianjin and Taiyuan. Shing Tung's father worked as a lecturer in China, although he had been a businessman before liberation in 1949. The Chows returned to Hong Kong in 1962 and Mr Chow went into a restaurant partnership only because he could not find suitable work in the academic field. As a northerner, who died several years ago, Mr Chow could speak neither Cantonese nor English.

Shing Tung has eleven other family members in Britain, including three younger brothers. His second brother, James, lives in Enfield and manages the family restaurant there. James is now married with two children. James's younger brother Shing Leung, 29 years old, is a computer programmer and is unmarried. Twenty-six-year-old Shing Chu is the youngest brother. After graduation from university, Shing Chu went to work for a firm of Chartered Accountants. Shing Tung's mother, Lee Man Wun, and 83-year-old grandmother are both living with James in Enfield.

For Shing Tung, the restaurant trade was not something he chose to go into. After doing his "A" levels, he completed three years at Middlesex Polytechnic on a Business Studies degree course. Because he did not finish his studies, he was unable to

Shing Tung Chow (right), his mother and younger brother, Shing Leung (left).

find suitable work. It was at the Polytechnic that Shing Tung met Shirley, his wife. Shirley is a Malaysian-born Chinese, whose father came to the UK in 1957 as a member of the British Armed Forces. Shing Tung and Shirley have been married for seven years and have a three-year-old son, Shaun. They now live in a private housing estate in Aylesbury. Previously, however, they lived above their restaurant in Tring.

Shirley Chow, Shing Tung's wife, with her son Fan Zheng (Shaun) in their new house in Aylesbury.

Shing Tung's grandmother (82 years old) who lives with her youngest grandson, Shing Chu, in Enfield. She is one of the few remaining women from China who have unnaturally small feet, as a result of binding at a very early age.

The Chan Family

Unlike the Wans and Chows, the Chan family is not involved in the catering business. Twenty-nine-year-old Alfred Chan works as a Chinese community worker in Edinburgh today. He came to Britain from the New Territories town of Tsuen Wan, Hong Kong, in 1975. Alfred's experience working as a psychiatric nurse in Hong Kong influenced his decision to come to Britain: "I could not believe the things I saw. It was there I had the experience of how human beings could do such nasty things to other human beings." As his qualifications were not recognized in Britain, Alfred had to sit for the U.K. exams to practise as a Registered Mental Nurse. Alfred later registered for a social work degree, making him the most educated member of the family.

In 1979 Alfred married Alice Lai Hing, his childhood girlfriend, who had come to Britain with him four years earlier. Alice is a qualified nurse, but works in the insurance business in Edinburgh. They have an eighteen-months-old son called Kwan Yu. The Chans live in Penicuik, in a small house rented from a housing association.

Alice and Alfred Chan hosting a meal in honour of the author. Eating out is a popular pastime amongst the Chinese.

Alfred's and Alice's family are all still in Hong Kong. Unlike the Chows and Wans, Alfred and Alice came to Britain without the support of an existing network of relatives or friends. Alfred's parents, who are both retired, now live in a government stage two resettlement block in the New Territories town of Tsuen Wan. They were born in Chiuyong in Guangdong province and migrated to Hong Kong in 1949. Mr Chan, who was a high-ranking officer in the Chinese Nationalist Army (Kuomintang), found a job as a clerk in the Hong Kong government service. Mrs Chan, who had only an elementary education, worked for years as a kitchen help in a factory, to help support the family.

Alfred has two older sisters, a younger brother and three younger sisters. Today Sun Kim and Sun Lin, the two elder sisters, are housewives. Cheung Kan, the brother, works as a checker at Hong Kong's largest container terminal. Of Alfred's younger sisters, Sun Chu, who is 25 years old, is a kindergarten teacher. Twenty-three-year-old Sun Fung is a foreman in a factory and the youngest, Sun Yi, is studying for her "A" levels.

An Established Migration Network

The most recent wave of migration from Hong Kong started in the early 1950s, some ten years before David Wan's and Shing Tung Chow's fathers came to Britain. This flow of Chinese migrants was related directly to the take-off of the Chinese restaurant trade. Chinese restaurants were beginning to become popular already during the Second World War. By this time, a number of ex-seamen who stayed on in this country moved into the catering business.

The restaurant "revolution" was novel in one respect. Previously, the early Chinatown restaurants catered for Chinese ship crews and students. But now, changing diets and conventions about eating-out in Britain increased the demand for Chinese food from the host community itself. Compared with some of the "up-market" eating establishments at the time, Chinese restaurants were places where most people could afford to eat.

Many of the Hong Kong Chinese who came in the 1950s and 1960s relied on contacts already established in Britain to find employment. These contacts were often brothers, uncles, cousins, fellow-villagers or friends. In a sense, the foothold established by these relatives and friends facilitated the passage of the newcomers. Mr Wan was

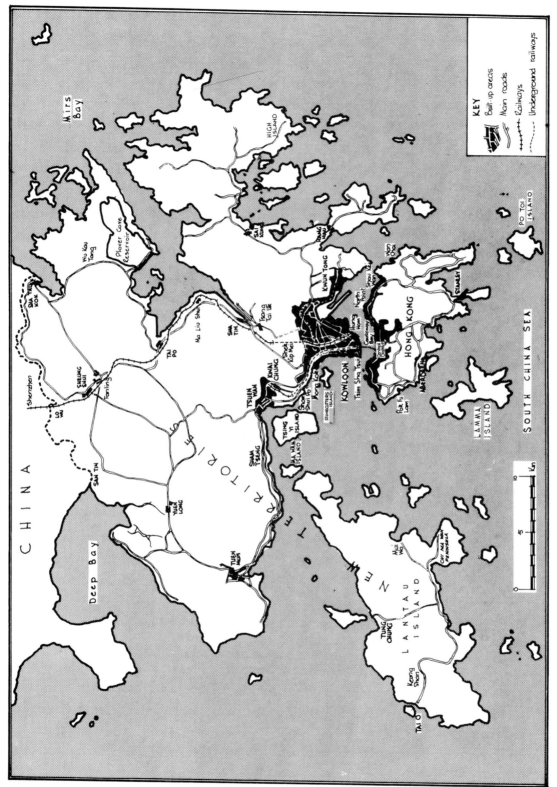

Hong Kong and the New Territories.

The Shanghai restaurant, Greek Street, London, 1939.

persuaded to come to Britain by a friend, also from the New Territories, Hong Kong. Mr Chow came to Britain in 1966, specifically to join his partner in a restaurant venture in London. In another sense, those Chinese who had successfully moved into the catering trade provided a model of success for those back in Hong Kong who were thinking of migrating. As "strangers" here, they demonstrated the feasibility of running a profitable enterprise in a foreign land.

Most of the newcomers arriving in the 1950s were young, unmarried men. The married ones left their wives at home and came here alone. This pattern was logical, in that the male migrants planned to spend

only a limited number of years in Britain, working hard and saving profusely, until they had enough to return home to a comfortable retirement. As will be clearer later, success for the Chinese also meant bringing a good "name" and reputation to their family, clan and ancestors. Undoubtedly, then, the economic motive was primary for most Chinese migrants going abroad. Shing Tung Chow recalled that Britain represented a land of "good living" for many Hong Kong Chinese. Shing Tung's father had no regrets about leaving Hong Kong for Britain. As Shing Tung put it: "You see, in people's eyes, Britain is a paradise. Just like people in China thinking Hong Kong is a paradise." News of the success of the early Chinese restauranteurs confirmed this vision of a land of "milk and honey".

So, whereas Chinese immigration to the USA was based on a contract labour recruitment system, those coming to Britain in the 1950s and 1960s were part of an informal system of chain migration, in which the newcomers were provided with initial accommodation and employment either by their relatives already in Britain or by their employers. This was not the case with Mr Wan, however, as he had to pay for his own air passage to London and no accommodation was provided for him by his first employer. Generally speaking, though, it was quite common for male restaurant workers to be found accommodation, either above the restaurant or in rooms let by the restaurant proprietor. Even when the migrants had to find their own accommodation, many would rely on information from relatives and friends. This was confirmed in a recent housing survey in Liverpool, which showed that a high proportion of Chinese in private rented accommodation had Chinese as landlords.

Tsuen Wan emerged as a new town in the 1960s. By 1989 it is reckoned that the population will have risen to 900,000.

The Home Villages

Circumstances in Britain enabled Chinese from Hong Kong to come to work here. But, also, pressures facing the rural folk in the New Territories in Hong Kong encouraged them to leave. Many able-bodied villagers had great difficulty in earning a decent living in the New Territories countryside, and this, coupled with the opportunity to make good in Europe, made migration overseas a realistic alternative.

The Chow family were originally from north China, although they spent several years in Hong Kong before coming to Britain. Shing Tung's father migrated to Britain for economic reasons. He simply could not find a suitable job in Hong Kong. Shing Tung's grandfather was a wealthy farmer who had been able to afford a good education for his son in the old China. Before going to Hong Kong, the Chows, managed to accumulate some money by trading items in short supply with the Japanese. Japan in the 1930s had occupied parts of China, with the intention of annexing parts of the country. The Chows, therefore, are not typical of most of the

Hong Kong migrants, who came from the rural New Territories.

Alfred Chan was born in Tsuen Wan, which today is a satellite town in the New Territories. His family only arrived in Hong Kong in 1949. Alfred regards his family as working-class. Unlike the Cantonese villagers in the New Territories, Alfred's family speak a native Chao Chou dialect.

David Wan's family have been in Hong Kong for several generations already. Like many of the New Territories migrants here, they came from a small kinship or lineage village, Cheung Lek Mei, where every family had the same surname. According to David, his ancestral village was more of a hamlet, with only six households. In David's own words, his father came to Britain to "make good". In fact, Mr Wan was the first member of the village to migrate abroad. Living conditions were certainly spartan. David recalled his early childhood: "We had no electricity at all. My family was very poor at the time. As farmers we grew rice, raised a few pigs and had a small tangerine orchard." At the age of six, David moved with his family to the nearby market town of Sha Tin. His father, who by then was working in London, sent money home for the removal expenses.

The Wans, like other Cantonese, consider themselves to be the original settlers of Guangdong province in southern China. Many of the Cantonese came from "single-lineage" villages, where all the male members share a common surname and trace their direct line of descent to a founding ancestor. Lineages are also property-owning units, based on land set aside by wealthy predecessors. Two or more

Today, the only remaining building in David Wan's village of Cheung Lek Mei is used as a vehicle repair shop.

A single-lineage village, Hunan province, South China.

Hakka women, New Territories, Hong Kong.

lineages with the same surname formed a clan. In the New Territories, there are five great Cantonese clans, namely the Tang, Hau, Pang, Liu and Man. Many of their members now reside in Britain. Generally speaking, these influential clans occupied the best land located in the north western part of the New Territories.

The *Hakka* tended to live in smaller villages, some with more than one surname or lineage group. As a distinctive group with their own dialect, the *Hakka* are said to have originated in Shandong province, north China. However, because they could be found all over China, they were known as "guest people".

In the old days, they were distinguished by their refusal to have the feet of their women bound. It was common practice, at the time, for wealthy and educated families to bind the feet of young girls, so that, as they grew up, they would have small, lotus-like feet which were considered beautiful. Footbinding was extremely painful and must also have prevented women from running away from their husband's household.

The *Hakka* were discriminated against in the old China. In the south, they were allocated a restricted quota of candidates who were allowed to take the Imperial system of exams to become registered scholars and government officials. As late-comers, the *Hakka* arrived in the New Territories several hundred years ago. Because most of the rich, fertile land was already in the hands of Cantonese farmers, the *Hakka* occupied the poorer mountainous areas on the eastern part of the New Territories, such as the Sai Kung peninsula. For the *Hakka*, in these mountainous villages, the difficulty of eking out even a modest living was a compelling force for the able-bodied to seek jobs in the city or even abroad.

Poverty itself was not really the cause of migration for the large Cantonese clans. Up until the 1940s, Cantonese farmers grew largely rice on their land. The Communist victory in mainland China then hit the New Territories agriculture in several respects. For a start, mainland farmers were able to supply Hong Kong with livestock products at a lower cost than New Territories farmers. Imported rice from Thailand and Burma was also cheaper and of a higher quality than that grown in Hong Kong.

The 1950s also saw a huge influx of peasant refugees from Guangdong province. Many rented

Refugee vegetable-growers from mainland China have built their own make-shift huts on rented land in the New Territories.

small plots of land from established villagers, on which they built small wooden houses and made a living, growing vegetables and rearing poultry. This "vegetable revolution" changed the occupational structures of the New Territories countryside. Those with fertile land found it more profitable to rent it to the refugee farmers for vegetable growing. Others found their incomes diminishing in the face of competition. The New Territories farmers' lack of contacts in urban Hong Kong made emigration abroad a more attractive alternative. The presence of some kinsmen already in Europe made the migration a reality.

It should be pointed out that not all the Chinese from Hong Kong came from these villages. Indeed, a considerable number migrated from urban areas and towns, as did Alfred Chan and the Chow family.

Arrivals of Wives and Family Dependants

As mentioned earlier, most of the male migrants who came to Britain 20-30 years ago were single. The unmarried migrants would save up for the first few years and find a wife when they returned to Hong Kong for a visit. By the early 1960s, an increasing number of male migrants were secure enough economically and felt sufficiently confident to ask the wives, children and, in some cases, elderly parents to join them. By this time, a number of Chinese restaurant workers had acquired their own small restaurant or take-away and so it made good sense for their families to come over to help out in the business. The tightening-up of immigration control through successive Immigration Acts also persuaded many Chinese of the need to call for their families to join them in Britain. The peak of family immigration was between 1963-73. This period saw the development of Chinese associations and societies, some specifically to cater for the growing educational and welfare needs of the community.

Those wives and mothers who did not help their husbands in the take-away business, or find jobs themselves as kitchen assistants in Chinese restaurants, stayed at home to look after the children. Many of them, however, did home-sewing on a piece-work basis, for wholesalers in the rag trade. Their living rooms, therefore, were not only a play-area for the children, but also a bustling clothing workshop. David Wan's sister-in-law, when not helping out at the take-away, would stay at home and do home-sewing.

As we shall see, the arrival of the migrants' wives and children was of tremendous importance in determining the growth of the Chinese community in Britain. Firstly, it enabled the expansion of Chinese take-aways as family businesses. It also created an awareness amongst the host population of the Chinese as a minority group in this society. Chinese children could now be found in British schools and Chinese families were moving into council housing. Family emigration also gradually changed the relationship of the original migrants to their home villages. With their families joining them, many migrants began to think in terms of settling down in Europe.

Not Just Waiters and Chefs

The Chinese in Britain are by no means a homogenous community. Besides those in the catering trade from Hong Kong, Chinese from Malaysia, Singapore and other parts of South East Asia are well-represented in Britain. Unlike the primarily Cantonese speakers from Hong Kong, most of the Chinese from South East Asia speak

Hokkien, the native dialect of Fujian province, Chao Chou and Mandarin. There are also a number of mainland Chinese living here, some for a considerable time already.

Although a number of the Chinese from South East Asia opened up restaurants serving Malaysian-style cuisine, many of them are in the professions such as law, accountancy and medicine. There is also a huge population of Chinese students and nurses in Britain, probably numbering 20–30,000. Most of them are from South East Asia, although a number are from urban parts of Hong Kong, like Alfred Chan. Until recently, many of the student nurses stayed on to work in the National Health Service after finishing their training. Now, immigration regulations have effectively stopped this practice.

Perhaps as many as 50 per cent of the Chinese in Britain are Cantonese from Hong Kong. Another 30 per cent are *Hakka* Chinese, with the remainder coming from South East Asia, mainland China, Taiwan and other parts of the world. Although it is a generalization, the Cantonese are said to have settled in London and the south, whereas the *Hakka* speakers are concentrated in the Midlands and north. To a large extent, the area of settlement was determined by the demands of the catering trade.

4

From Gourmet Restaurant to Sweet and Sour "Chippy"

It was the openings created in the catering trade which provided the impetus for large-scale Chinese migration to Britain. Therefore, the Chinese tended to settle in areas offering relevant job opportunities. Initially, these would have been places where relatives and friends had already established themselves.

The 1981 Census records Britain's Chinese population as 154,363. This figure includes heads of households (usually fathers) born in Hong Kong, China, Malaysia and Singapore and their dependants. Excluded are those household heads born in Britain or other parts of the world. In places such as London and Liverpool, where there are long-established Chinese communities, the total Chinese population would be somewhat larger if the British-born parents were to be included in the figures.

Nearly half of Britain's Chinese population are settled in London and the south east. However, as we shall see, the search for new locations to open restaurants, coupled with the trend towards setting up take-aways, saw the Chinese moving to other provincial towns and cities. Outside London, the next biggest concentration of Chinese is in the north west, which has a Chinese population exceeding 14,000. Today, every small town or seaside resort has a Chinese restaurant or take-away. Shing Tung Chow's restaurant, "Waterfall", is the only Chinese restaurant in Tring.

In London, the Chinese have settled in over 30 metropolitan boroughs, although Camden and Westminster have the largest Chinese populations. Most of the authentic Cantonese cuisines are located in Soho Chinatown, whilst Chinese take-aways have sprouted up in the suburbs or outside the West End.

David Wan's parents run the take-away "Suey Hong" in Bethnal Green, just a stone's throw away from their flat.

Categories of Immigrant

Most of the New Territories migrants came to Britain under the voucher system, provided under the Commonwealth Immigration Act 1962. In the majority of cases, restaurant workers were issued with a category "A" voucher, which was valid for a range of unskilled and semi-skilled jobs. David Wan's father came to Britain under this scheme. The rules required the employer to apply for a voucher on the worker's behalf. This gave an in-built advantage to those migrants with relatives and friends already in Britain, since many of the employers were fellow-villagers or kinsmen.

The 1960s, however, saw a new category of Chinese immigrant to Britain. First of all, not all the Chinese from Hong Kong were born in the territory. In fact, a considerable proportion of Hong Kong's population is made up of refugees and emigrants from mainland China. In the 1960s a growing number of China-born migrants came to Britain, to fill vacancies in restaurants. Many were natives of Guangdong province and, as "aliens", they did not qualify for vouchers, which were restricted to British passport-holders. Between 1963-73 probably as many as 10,000 Chinese aliens found employment in Britain, after work permits had been obtained for them. Unlike the voucher-holders, not all of the Chinese "aliens" came to work in restaurants. Of the 1,335 who arrived n 1969, 375 found jobs in hospitals and in private industry.

Sadly, many of the Chinese "aliens" who did find

"Waterfall" Chinese restaurant in Enfield, Middlesex, a Peking-style cuisine, owned by the Chow family and managed by James Chow and his mother, Lee Man Wun.

James Chow (Shing Ming), second son of the Chow family, calculating the day's receipts at the family restaurant in Enfield.

work in Chinese restaurants were treated as "second-class" immigrants by the established restauranteurs from the New Territories. The "alien" workers had few contacts and relatives in Britain and were thus dependent on those Chinese who came under the voucher scheme for jobs. Generally speaking, the Chinese "aliens" had to work for wages lower than those paid to New Territories migrants. As relative newcomers, they were also allocated back-room menial jobs, such as kitchen hands, despite the fact that some of them, on paper, were skilled workers such as chefs.

The Organization of the Restaurant Trade

With hindsight, Shing Tung Chow agreed that, even if the immigration regulations did not confine the Chinese to catering work, it was still a convenient starting-point for those who came with nothing in their pockets.

In the Chinese restaurant trade, several forms of ownership are common. Small and medium-sized restaurants tend to be owned by a sole proprietor or family, or run as a partnership venture. The larger establishments are generally owned by wealthy Chinese proprietors who also own other restaurants in Britain and Europe.

At today's prices (1984), it would cost over £100,000 to set up a small Chinese restaurant in London's West End. Because of these prohibitive costs, it is common therefore for such establishments to be set up and run as a partnership. You will recall that Shing Tung's father came to Britain to work as a partner in a Chinese restaurant in Woolwich. Newcomers could, after several years' saving, accumulate enough money to invest in a partnership.

In general, most partnerships consist of kinsmen or fellow-villagers from home. The restaurant manager would normally be a senior partner, with a larger stake in the business than the waiters and meat-choppers. The chefs, as Shing Tung Chow explained, were either partners or the highest-paid employees. Experienced chefs these days in the top-class West End restaurants could earn over £250 per week. However, the long hours and hot kitchen surroundings were very exacting.

After a few years, the working partners would have built up sufficient capital to open their own restaurants or take-aways. This process leads to the proliferation of Chinese eating houses. It also enables

Chinese chefs at work in a Soho Chinese restaurant.

most Chinese to realize their aim of "being their own boss".

Although the majority of restaurants serving authentic Chinese food have a Cantonese-style cuisine, there are also a growing number of Peking-style restaurants in Britain today. Shing Tung Chow, whose restaurant in Tring serves Peking-style or northern Chinese specialities, thinks that Europeans are particularly keen on this type of cuisine. The majority of customers in most Peking-style restaurants, he says, are European and not Chinese. Many of the earlier Peking-style restaurants in Britain were set up by mainland Chinese who came here as refugees or immigrants shortly before or after the Communists came to power in 1949. Unlike their New Territories counterparts, these northern proprietors came from urban backgrounds and were either businessmen or scholars. Shing Tung's father is an example.

Today, Shing Tung looks after the restaurant in Tring, whilst his brother James runs the other family restaurant in Enfield. Shing Tung has been in the restaurant business for over ten years already. Because Shing Tung is married to a Malaysian Chinese and, unlike Hong Kong restaurant owners, does not have many dealings with Cantonese restaurant workers, he prefers employing Chinese from Malaysia as waiters. He also had no hesitation in employing several local white staff, as part-time waiters and bar attendants. As Shing Tung explained, the biggest headache for any restaurant owner is to find an experienced and motivated team of chefs. Until very recently, Shing Tung had a team of one chief chef and two assistants from Hong Kong. As in many other Peking-style restaurants, the staff are simply employees, with no partnership stake in the business.

Restaurant work is certainly hard work. On average, restaurant workers work 10-12 hours a day and six days a week. In the afternoon, they have several hours off, when they can either have a nap or pass the time in other ways. There are some fringe benefits, however. Tips, for example, are usually divided up according to some established formula. In many cases, senior staff receive a larger share of the receipts from tips. Kitchen staff do not always benefit from this pay-out either. Other benefits include the occasional supply of food which staff can take home to their families. All meals are also provided to restaurant staff in-between shifts in the morning, afternoon and late evening.

In the smaller towns, restaurant staff, particularly the chefs, are usually provided with accommodation by the owner. According to Shing Tung Chow, if the owner's family itself does not occupy the rooms above the restaurant, then in all likelihood they would be rented out to his staff. At present, the three chefs working at Shing Tung's restaurant in Tring all have rooms above the restaurant. In London, though, because of the high rents and strict zoning laws, restaurant workers live outside the Soho district. In some cases, the restaurant proprietors provide transport home for their staff after closing hours, which is often as late as midnight or 1.00 a.m.

Most of the Soho Chinese restaurants use the services of local Chinese accountants, of whom there are several, to keep their books and advise them on their dealings with the Inland Revenue. The Chinese restaurant trade is not unionized. In the past, the Transport and General Workers' Union has not made a concerted effort to woo Chinese restaurant workers. Not only is there a language barrier, but most Chinese catering establishments employ fewer than fifteen workers. The fact that many restaurants are run as partnerships means that the restaurant staff see themselves as both owner and worker at the same time. In general, however, it would be fair to say that many Chinese emigrants do not see themselves as workers whose interests are diametrically opposed to those of their employers. Furthermore, in some cases, their employer would be a relative or fellow villager. For many restaurant workers, being employed as a waiter is the first step on the way towards realizing their ambition to have their own establishment one day.

Having said that, though, harsh working conditions, such as long hours, poor wages and the deliberate avoidance of national insurance payments by some restaurant owners, have made some restaurant workers consider more militant ways of improving their situation. At the time of writing, discussions are underway amongst some Chinese workers to set up a Chinese trades union for catering workers. As mentioned earlier, the position of many China-born "aliens" is considerably less favourable in the restaurant hierarchy than that of the voucher-holders from the New Territories.

The Take-Away Explosion

The arrival of children and wives in the mid-1960s and 1970s particularly suited the expansion of Chinese take-aways. Whereas a restaurant worker would have had to find a huge amount of capital to buy his own restaurant, particularly in a large city like London or Birmingham, setting up a take-away was an attainable ambition. For a fraction of the costs, a Chinese family could set up and run their own take-away business in a small town or the suburbs of a city. Through sheer hard work and savings, therefore, many Chinese restaurant workers could raise their economic status from *kung* (worker) to *sheung* (businessman).

Although it is difficult to distinguish one take-away from another, there are basically two types of Chinese take-away establishment. One is the "Chop Suey" house, offering a range of adapted Chinese fast-food dishes thought to be palatable to Westerners' taste-buds. The word "Chop Suey" was invented by a Chinese chef in New York at the end of the nineteenth century, to refer to a Westernized dish made up of fried left-overs. The other type is a "Chinese chippy", where a Chinese family takes over a "Fish and Chip" shop and continues to offer the same items available at these "friers". In most cases, the menu is modified to also include a range of

Chinese fast-foods. In practice, however, most take-away establishments contain a mixture of both features.

The success of the take-aways can be shown in the figures. In the north west region, there are now around 500 Chinese "chippies", each offering a wide menu of 30-40 dishes, including the traditional fish and chips and meat pies. Having a broad menu is certainly one explanation for their popularity and success. Also, service is fast, and the food reasonably priced. Unlike other eating establishments, Chinese take-aways are open usually from mid-day to midnight, every day of the week. Operational costs are low for the family owners, who do not have to hire additional labour, and thus save a weekly wage bill. In some cases, the family will live in the spare rooms above the take-away shop, thus saving travel time and accommodation costs.

But how do things operate at David Wan's family take-away, the "Suey Hong"? David's parents are in catering because, in his own words, "they have no choice. My parents arrived with little English and their education in Hong Kong was disrupted by the war." The "Suey Hong" is open every day of the week, although Sundays is half-day opening, from 5.00 p.m. onwards. Like other take-aways, it is open on Chinese New Year, Christmas Day and other public holidays. In the past, David's father did the cooking, but because he is now better-off, he has employed two cooks for the kitchen. Despite this, the work is still very hard, according to David, who with his sister-in-law helps out at weekends. His brother, Kenneth, has started working full-time at the take-away since leaving college. When David was still at school, he would also work at the take-away on some evenings and at weekends.

Nearly all the customers to the "Suey Hong" are white. The menu, according to David, is "of a Chop Suey variety. Chop Suey is very mild and easily acceptable to the English palate. We also sell chips, as most customers like it." Authentic Chinese food is available in the West End restaurants. David thought that since proper Chinese cooking would involve more preparation and this increases the costs and waiting time, most take-aways would lose their customers by offering it. Chinese cooking is, of course, a culinary art. Great emphasis is placed on colour, texture and flavour in the presentation of each dish. At a non-festive occasion, a simple meal would consist of several dishes served all at once on the table. Soup would be served with the main dishes and not before. Unlike with European food, all the dinner guests are expected to try a little from all the dishes served. For a feast or banquet, say to celebrate a wedding, each of the dishes is specially prepared and they are served one at a time.

Success in the take-away business is sometimes bought at the cost of social isolation, excessively

The Wan family's take-away, the "Suey Hong", in London's East End.

Kenneth Wan substituting as the cook in his parents' take-away. Saturdays are particularly busy.

hard work and, in recent years, vulnerability to vandalism and racial harassment. For the many Chinese families running take-aways in small towns, their lives are work-dominated and often socially joyless. In many cases, there may be only two or three other Chinese families in the town. The London Chinese who run the Soho Quarter are different from their provincial cousins, whom they supply and service. Within Chinatown, the Soho Chinese have the confidence of numbers and an environment in which they feel at home. Social isolation for Chinese in the regions can lead to psycho-social problems, particularly for elderly Chinese women. The yearning for Chinese cultural activities can be illustrated by the fact that some Chinese restaurant workers in Scotland would travel up to 30 miles after work to see a Chinese film or to play *Mah Jeong* (a Chinese game with tiles) with friends.

Because of their dispersion, Chinese restaurants and take-aways have become easy targets of vandalism and violence. Because of language difficulties, most of these incidents go unreported. Some take-away owners in Merseyside, though, are known to have taken the law into their own hands in combating such harassment, by pouring boiling oil out of windows and installing high-voltage wires across window frames.

Saturation Point

Today, estimates suggest there are around 7,000 Chinese restaurants and take-aways in Britain. The last four years have witnessed a noticeable slowdown in the growth of the catering trade. Increasing competition amongst Chinese caterers, no doubt, has reduced profitability in some areas. The continuing recession has not helped matters either. Furthermore, the costs involved in setting up a restaurant or even a take-away are becoming prohibitive.

Since a number of restaurants have gone "up-market", eating out at these establishments has become a luxury. At the same time, those restaurants which have stood still and not re-decorated their dining room, or provided training for their waiters and up-graded their menu, have lost the patronage of those customers who have a more sophisticated appreciation of Chinese food. To be fair, immigration restrictions have also curbed the growth of restaurants in some cases, as labour shortages have pushed up wages and inhibited new restaurants from being set up.

Market saturation is the main reason why many chose to emigrate from Britain to Holland, Germany and France in the last decade. Holland alone has nearly 12,000 Hong Kong Chinese in the restaurant and catering trade. In most cases, the Hong Kong migrants would have acquired "patriality" or "the right to abode in the United Kingdom" before re-emigrating to Europe. This would then entitle them to work and live in the EEC countries, with minimum restrictions.

5

Chinatown,
"The Imperial City"

London's Chinatown, although minuscule in comparison with those in San Francisco and Vancouver, has a symbolic existence which outweighs its geographical size. In many ways, it serves as a symbol of the presence of the Chinese in Britain as a distinct ethnic group with its own language, culture and organizations.

It was only in the early 1960s that the area surrounding Gerrard Street in Soho took over as Chinatown from the Limehouse dock district. By this time, Liverpool's smaller Chinese Quarter had moved from Pitt Street to the neighbouring area encompassing Nelson Street and Great Georges Square. Since then, Soho Chinatown, known to the Chinese as "the Imperial City", has grown phenomenally. In 1965 there were only 20 Chinese restaurants and three Chinese groceries in Soho. Today, the district boasts 90-100 Chinese restaurants and countless other businesses.

For the Chinese living in the suburbs and small provincial towns, such as the Wans in Bethnal Green and the Chow family in Enfield and Aylesbury, the Chinese eating-houses in Soho serve as a major meeting place. Soho's shops and services also provide Chinese families with essential foods and other supplies for home and their own catering businesses. Much hustle and bustle takes place on Sundays, when Chinese families close their take-aways for half a day or when restaurant workers take their day off to take their families to Chinatown.

The picture painted of Chinatown, so far, is one where the Chinese rely on each other for a variety of services and business transactions. Alfred Chan, who is a community worker, feels that Chinatown is not a community of people with common interests but a "giant market place" where human encounters take place on a commercial basis. Walking through Soho Chinatown, Alfred explained: "In many ways we are a community. We are together for the community's interest. But the interest will mainly be for economic purposes. We are together not because of our race or political reasons but purely for economic interests."

Although to some extent this is the case, the proliferation of Chinese shops and agencies do provide an essential service to the Chinese. Furthermore, as we shall see, the growth of Chinese associations both within and outside Chinatown has been in response to a growing need for a variety of activities catering to Chinese families. These Chinese associations serve as a vital focal point for Chinese in small towns or cities, where there is no large concentration of Chinese. Even in Edinburgh, as Alfred Chan admits, where there are 2,500 Chinese inhabitants, the sense of a community is missing, because of the absence of a central Chinatown district.

The Life and Soul of Chinatown

To Londoners with a passion for Chinese food, Soho Chinatown is a place to get the gastric juices going. In the last decade, however, Chinatown has grown into a self-sufficient enclave catering to an immense range of needs. Diversification within the catering trade has seen the growth of Chinese supermarkets and provision shops. There are now also Chinese fish and vegetable wholesalers, who sell to retailers in Chinatown. Outside Soho, food processing such as bean-sprout and springroll factories have provided jobs for Chinese.

One of the largest Chinese supermarkets in Gerrard Street, Soho.

A new Chinese art and crafts shop which opened in Gerrard Street in 1983.

Below, a Chinese shop in Soho selling martial arts equipment and uniforms. Above, a Chinese barber's shop.

Jade Travel in Wardour Street, London W1, is owned by members of the Man clan.

The growth in non-catering trades has been even greater. Walking along Gerrard Street, Lisle Street, Wardour Street and even Shaftesbury Avenue, one will find Chinese travel agencies, printing houses, arts and crafts shops and bookshops. Chinatown has its own barbers, social clubs, accountancy firms and cinemas. Recently, a number of video-hire shops have sprouted up, offering cheap rental of Chinese movies and soap operas from Hong Kong.

One of the oldest art and crafts bookshops in Gerrard Street is "Hong Kong Cultural Services", which is owned by Mr K.C. Cheung and his son. The Cheungs were originally from Shenzhen in Guangdong province, China. Chinese customers, according to Mr K.C. Cheung, tended to buy newspapers, magazines and short stories. Europeans were generally keen on art and crafts, such as jade and ivory ornaments and ceramic ware. In the past, Mr Cheung's shop had been a centre for disseminating news from home. Mr Cheung also used to employ a Chinese bi-lingual advisory worker, who helped Chinese workers with legal, welfare and immigration enquiries.

The Chinese also have their own newspapers. *Sing Tao Yat Po* is the largest Chinese daily, with a UK circulation well over 10,000. The newspaper's European edition is printed in Uxbridge. *Wah Kiu Yat Po* is another newspaper with a European edition. These newspapers have to compete with those flown from Hong Kong and mainland China, such as *Ta Kung Po, Wen Wei Po* and *Ren Min Ri Bao*. In general, the newspapers serve as an essential link between the migrants in Britain and their home countries. The emphasis seems to be changing today, with the recent establishment of a Europe-wide Chinese daily, *Europe Journal*, which is printed in Paris. The focus of this newspaper is on Europe as the adopted home of over 600,000 overseas Chinese.

Soho even has its own Chinese doctors, whose surgeries are close to Chinatown. Because of difficulties in communicating with their local GPs, many Chinese living in the suburbs would visit these Chinese-speaking doctors, despite the long journey. Western medicine is generally accepted by the Chinese today, although many still place their trust in the traditional methods of herbalism, acupuncture and massage therapy.

The Soho Chinese also have their own practitioners of traditional medicine. Mr T.K. Li, whose clinic is right in Gerrard Street, is one of the more established practitioners. Mr Li's patients, mainly Chinese, come from all parts of the country. Besides treating with an infinite variety of herbs from China, Mr Li also concocts his own tablets

One of the two Chinese cinemas in Soho. In the centre, Mr K.C. Cheung, proprietor of *Hong Kong Cultural Services,* whose shop is next door.

Mrs Cheung Lu Meng Ling, a Shanghai trained acupuncturist with her own clinic in Soho.

from specially prepared recipes. His patients are treated for a variety of ailments, ranging from psycho-somatic illnesses to arthritis.

More and more Europeans are turning to traditional Chinese medicine for treatment, according to Mrs Cheung Lu Meng Ling, a Shanghai-trained acupuncturist, who recently opened a clinic in Shaftesbury Avenue. Acupuncture is perhaps the most commonly known method of treatment in Chinese medicine. Basically, it involves the insertion and rotation of a number of small, sterilized needles in certain key points of the body. The aim is to stimulate the body's energy-flow (*chi*) back to a healthy equilibrium.

For those Chinese interested to know what the future holds, a visit would be made to the Chinese fortune-teller (sooth-sayer) in Gerrard Street. By simply examining a client's face and palms, the fortune-teller would make predictions about proposed marriages, travel prospects and general luck.

Chinese Pastimes

Popular with the older Chinese is the Sunday pastime of *yum cha* (tea and small eats) at one of Soho's Chinese restaurants serving *dim sum* (small delicacies). David Wan's parents visit Chinatown regularly on Sundays to meet friends over a *dim sum* meal. Mrs Wan uses this opportunity to buy provisions from the Chinese supermarket for their take-away. After lunch, David's father would visit his friend's house for a game of *mah jeong*, a Chinese card game akin to rummy, involving the use of plastic tiles. Although the game is played for money, *mah jeong* is more a traditional pastime than a form of gambling for high stakes.

Watching a Chinese movie is still a popular pastime for Chinese families and youngsters. There are two Chinese cinemas in Soho showing *kung fu* films, romances and thrillers from Hong Kong and Taiwan. In addition, the Empire and Odeon Leicester Square normally show a Chinese film as a midnight show at weekends. In recent years, however, the attendance at Chinese cinemas has fallen. Alfred Chan thought that the availability of Chinese movies on video has made it more convenient for families and friends to stay at home to watch the film. Many Chinese families have video recorders, and cassette rentals are extremely cheap.

The lack of recreational facilities is certainly a problem affecting the elderly and the young. Many retired workers are content to pass the time reading Chinese newspapers and magazines. Even the young enjoy reading. David Wan's brother, Kenneth, enjoys reading Chinese short stories and more specialized journals dealing with Chinese herbs. Table tennis, badminton and football are popular sports for the younger Chinese.

Gambling

Undoubtedly, the main pastime is gambling. For the male restaurant workers and owners, gambling is not only a recreational activity, it also offers a means of "striking it rich". A lucky session would enable them to pay off debts, buy a stake in a partnership or even return home with some capital.

There are over 20 Chinese gambling clubs in London and other major cities. Gerrard Street alone houses 7-8 of these dens, in basement premises guarded by well-built bouncers schooled in the martial arts. These clubs are exclusively for Chinese, mainly men. Although a certain amount of gambling takes place in some restaurants after hours, the gambling dens are usually packed in the afternoon hours between 3-5 pm, when restaurant workers

Well-known soho gambling den, the Cheung Shing Club in Gerrard Street, London W1.

have a few hours off.

Fan tan, a form of roulette, and *pai kau* (Chinese dominoes) are the most popular games played in the clubs. *Fan tan* is usually played with buttons or beans. Participants place bets on the number of buttons or beans left under an upturned bowl after they have been gradually removed four at a time. *Pai kau* is played with Chinese dominoes and the rules are akin to Russian poker. The game is played with a maximum of eight persons, although bystanders are allowed to bet on players' hands. In both games, the club owners levy a percentage on the winnings. The stakes can be very high, although there is usually a betting limit imposed. There have been reports, however, of restaurants changing hands around the gambling table.

Another popular game is *pak kap piu*, literally "pidgeon lottery", which is a form of bingo, Chinese style. The game is usually played twice daily and participants have to select a group of Chinese characters out of a possible pool of 80. The results are declared several hours later, when the winning combination of characters is posted on the wall in the gambling dens.

Chinese community workers like Alfred Chan are critical of the illegal gambling dens, since these sometimes become enmeshed in the intrigues of the Chinese underworld, where rival gangs contend to control these profitable outlets. Commenting on a recent bombing incident involving one of these Soho clubs, Alfred said: "It's a very serious problem at the moment. The petrol bomb incident in Soho where 7 people were killed has a direct link with illegal gambling dens."

The attitude of the police to illegal gambling has not been uniform. In some cases, they have raided the clubs, only to find the club owners returning to business as usual after paying the fines. In other cases, the police have tolerated this illegality, seeing it as a cultural trait of the Chinese confined essentially to their own ethnic group.

In recent years, the possibility has been officially mooted of legalizing Chinese gambling, either by bringing existing clubs "above ground", with strict controls, or by introducing Chinese games in existing casinos. Chinese gamblers are already frequenting casinos and up to 30 per cent of the clientele in some West End casinos is Chinese.

Easily forgotten, however, is the social importance of the gambling clubs. They function as a meeting place for male workers and also serve as an informal "job centre" for those looking for work. In some clubs, illicit money-lending also takes place, often at high rates of interest.

The Earliest Chinese Associations

Chinese associations in Britain generally combine the functions of organizing social and cultural activities for their members and representing the Chinese in their contacts with the host society. The early associations provided a sense of social cohesion for the Chinese seamen, and the traditional practice of mutual help was translated into a myriad of activities supported by the associations.

In one respect, the early associations differed from the ones which were established in the 1960s and '70s. For example, the oldest association in London, the Hui Tong Kung Sheung Association, was established in 1907 in the East End, to provide a place where Chinese workers could meet without being ridiculed and humiliated by the English. The early seamen suffered a considerable amount of discrimination, compared with the newcomers from Hong Kong.

Aside from providing *fongs* (meeting places) to shield members from open humiliation, the Hui Tong Association was set up to promote mutual help amongst the overseas Chinese and help improve their living conditions. In the past, the association assisted Chinese seamen to negotiate better working conditions. It also provided a variety of welfare benefits covering sickness and death. Those who were sick in hospital were visited by members of the association. Retired workers returning to China were also assisted with their passage. An important function of these early associations was to make funeral arrangements for members who died in Britain. The Chinese have always placed great emphasis on a proper burial and so the associations did ease anxieties in this respect. The Hui Tong Association also visited the graves of early seamen at certain festivals, such as *Ching Ming* in the spring.

Membership of the Hui Tong was open to male workers and shopkeepers. Today, the association exists largely as a social and gambling club in the East End. It has also changed its name to Ching Yee Association and most of its members are now restaurant workers and other Chinese in the catering trade.

The second oldest Chinese organization in London is the Chinese Mutual Aid Workers Club, founded in 1920 with the same aims as the Hui Tong Association. The club financed its activities not only from membership subscriptions but also from levies on gambling which took place on its premises. It also received donations, and the large donors had their portraits hung in a ceremonial remembrance hall. In the early 1960s, the club moved to new premises in the West End, with a TV room, dining hall, gambling room and dormitory for homeless Chinese. Until very recently, the club showed films from China and organized a variety of outings for Chinese children. It also ran Chinese-language classes for the children of workers. At one time, nearly 200 children were enrolled in these classes.

Liverpool also had its own early Chinese

The Chi Kung Tong (Chinese Masonic Lodge) in Nelson Street, Liverpool.

A memorial erected by Chi Kung Tong in Everton Cemetery in memory of all Chinese who died in Britain.

associations. The Chi Kung Tong (Chinese Masonic Lodge) has an eighty-year history in Merseyside. The lodge was a branch of the Chinese secret society or Triad, known as the *Hung Mun Hui*. In the past, the lodge's members, mostly seamen, were provided with a variety of services and benefits. The lodge found work for its members, provided a safe meeting place for them, and also mediated in disputes between the Chinese. An important function was to make funeral arrangements for members who died in Britain. In the Chinese sections of Anfield and Everton cemeteries, the lodge had placed two epitaphs, in memory of all those Chinese who died in Britain. Today, the lodge's membership has shrunk and its activity is largely confined to providing hostel accommodation for elderly homeless Chinese men.

Another old association is the Sze Yap Association in Liverpool. This was a district organization for fellow countrymen from the Sze Yap district in Guangdong province. Before the last war, the majority of the Cantonese in Britain were from the Sze Yap district in China.

Rather than joining these associations in large numbers, the post-war Chinese from the New Territories preferred instead to set up their own associations. To some extent, the two groups of migrants had different horizons and experiences. The seamen, as old-timers, were from mainland China, whereas the newcomers came from Hong Kong half a century later. Unlike the seamen, the New Territories Chinese, in most cases, had jobs arranged for them in the restaurant trade. Compared to the old-timers, their earnings were large. Many of the seamen initially thought that these *san tsai* (new boys) from Hong Kong were arrogant and "standoffish". More significant was the fact that the newcomers were less exposed to racial discrimination than the earlier seamen, as they found employment in a self-contained niche, which did not involve competing with whites for jobs.

Post-War Chinese Associations

Most of the present-day associations were formed within ten years of large-scale Chinese immigration to Britain. The period of family emigration beginning in the mid-1960s saw the Chinese community trying to respond, from being solely concerned with the welfare of male migrants and their ties to the homeland, to helping the Chinese adjust to life in Britain.

One organization which has made considerable efforts in the last few years to cater to the needs of the Chinese community is the Chinese Chamber of Commerce. The Chamber has over a thousand members all over Britain. It was originally set up to represent the interests of Chinese traders and restauranteurs in Britain. However, besides helping with matters such as company registration, the Chamber has an impressive record in promoting the welfare of the Chinatown Chinese.

The Chamber is at the forefront in the effort to promote Chinese culture, especially amongst the second generation Chinese. Together with the London Chinese Protestants Association, it organized in the summer of 1983 a series of afternoon cultural forums, at its Frith Street premises, for restaurant workers and their families. This consisted of films, magic shows, folk dances and general discussions. Chinese mother-tongue maintenance is also very important to the Chamber, which happens to run the largest Chinese school in Europe, with a pupil enrolment of 900 schoolchildren. As we shall see in the next chapter, Chinese parents are keen to ensure that their children do not "forget their origins" and ancestral culture.

To help the Chinese learn English, however, was also a priority for the Chamber. In the 1970s, attempts were made to organize English-language classes for Chinese waiters, in co-operation with ILEA, under the Neighbourhood English Classes scheme. These efforts were not successful, primarily because of the unsocial hours worked by the waiters who were often too exhausted to study in their free time.

Other activities initiated by the Chamber included a campaign to improve hygiene standards in Chinese restaurants and lobbying the Home Office for more flexible immigration regulations governing the entry of migrant workers and their dependants. In the early 1970s, the Chamber was actively involved in preventing the City of Westminster from approving a plan to demolish the buildings in Gerrard Street, for the purposes of re-developing Soho and erecting an extension to the Telephone Exchange. This would have meant an end to Chinatown and the creation of major unemployment amongst Chinese workers.

Primary-school children attending a mother-tongue Chinese class run by the Chinese Chamber of Commerce in Soho, London.

In the last few years, the Chamber has tried, with other organizations, to work with as many other Chinese associations as possible in an attempt to unite the Chinese community in Britain. The end result was the setting up of the Federation of Chinese Associations in 1980, as an umbrella organization representing over 30 Chinese groups in Britain.

One organization to belong is the London Chinatown Chinese Association, set up in May 1978. Although the association is concerned with encouraging the development of Chinese businesses in Soho, it also recognizes the need for a variety of services for the Chinese working in Chinatown. With the help of an Urban Aid grant, the association set up a Chinese community centre in July 1980, providing a free consultative service for the Chinese in Soho. At the centre, two Chinese social workers offer advice on a host of issues relating to housing, immigration law, welfare entitlements and taxation matters. The association is also responsible for organizing the annual Chinese New Year celebrations in Chinatown (see next chapter).

So far, the associations described are modern, in that they represent a particular occupational grouping or distinct geographical community. The Chinese from the New Territories brought with them, however, more traditional organizations, such as clan associations. Yet, compared with other parts of the world where the Chinese settled, these traditional associations based on a common surname, dialect or district did not play a central role in the daily life of Britain's Chinese. Unlike in the United States and South East Asia, the economic gap that Chinese workers filled in Britain was not controlled by any specific association.

Although many of the Chinese in Britain belong to a number of Cantonese and *Hakka* clans, only three clan associations have been set up over the years. The earliest was Cheungs' Clansmen Charity Association (Europe), which was founded in 1965 and has a Europe-wide membership of 300 today. The Cheungs were originally from Shenzhen in Guangdong province. Before the last war, many of their members crossed the border into Hong Kong. As a kinship organization, the Cheungs get together annually for a banquet during the mid-autumn Moon Festival in September. The association currently runs its own mother-tongue classes at weekends. Tuition is free and attendance is open to all Chinese children, including those with other surnames.

The largest clan association in Britain is the Mans' Clansmen Association, which has a Europe-wide membership of 1,500. Because most of the Mans are scattered all over Europe, it was only in 1976 that the association was formed. Primarily, it has concerned itself with recreational activities and outings for its members. Every autumn it organizes a trip to Hong Kong for its members. Their visit coincides with Chung Yang Festival, which is traditionally a time to pay homage to one's ancestors.

The other clan organization is that of the Pangs, established in 1968. Although it has permanent premises in Lisle Street, Soho, the association is largely symbolic, with few activities other than welcoming new arrivals from Pang villages in the New Territories.

Middle-class Chinese also have their own associations. One of the oldest is the Hong Kong Overseas Professionals Association (HOPA), set up in 1971 to promote social and professional contacts amongst professional people mainly from Hong Kong. HOPA has several hundred members in Britain, many of whom are doctors, nurses, accountants, teachers and engineers.

In April 1983, the London Chinatown Lions' Club held its inaugural meeting in Soho. Most of its 30 founding members are businessmen or in the professions. The Chinatown Lions' Club is part of the Lions International network, which is the largest charitable-service organization in the world.

The main weakness of the West End Chinese organizations is that they do not cater to the Chinese living in other parts of the country or even in the London suburbs. David Wan's family has not joined any of these clubs or associations, since they do not work in Chinatown. As described in Chapter Nine, this need has been met by an increasing number of local Chinese community organizations set up and run by educated Chinese who have no direct links with the restaurant trade.

Although the Chinese are relatively new to Edinburgh, having first moved there in 1970, there are already four voluntary associations providing educational and recreational activities for the local Chinese. According to Alfred Chan, Edinburgh's Chinese are made up of three distinct groups. The first group, consisting of 300 or so Chinese, come from the island of Ap Chau, which is part of Hong Kong. The rest come from the New Territories and from the urban areas of Hong Kong. The Edinburgh

Inaugural meeting of Chinatown Lions' Club in Soho. Rev. Stephen Ng, chairman (standing), is also the minister of the Chinese Rhenish Church in West London.

Hong Kong Chinese Association was the first to be established. Today, it provides a variety of recreational activities at its Dublin Street premises, such as table tennis and a reading and TV room. It also sponsors football matches and organizes group tours for Chinese holiday-makers.

In the late 1970s, Chinese associations were established by restauranteurs, shopkeepers and professionals in other cities, such as the Chinese Midlands Association in Birmingham and the Kung Sheung Chinese Community of Manchester.

Political Affiliations

Britain's Chinese generally tend to avoid actively identifying either with Communist China or with the nationalist Kuomintang government in Taiwan. The Chinese Embassy and its rival Taiwanese Free Trade Centre are engaged in a propaganda war to win the "hearts and minds" of the overseas Chinese. Free literature and bulletins and all kinds of films are regularly distributed to Chinese clubs and societies. The Guanghua Bookshop in Soho stocks only books, magazines and newspapers from mainland China, whereas other Chinese bookshops in Gerrard Street sell Taiwanese and Hong Kong publications. It is true to say, though, that, whatever their political convictions, Britain's Chinese are tremendously proud of China's emergence as a world power.

The largest pro-China group in London is the Kung Ho Association in Meard Street. Although most of its leaders are openly pro-Communist, most of its 300 members joined out of nationalistic pride for the motherland's achievements. Shing Tung Chow's mother is a member of Kung Ho's women's committee. The committee's main function is to organize celebrations, such as on International Women's Day on 8 March. Kung Ho was set up in 1963, to assist Chinese workers in their dealings with the host society and to arrange English classes for restaurant workers. Today, the association is involved in a variety of activities, from running a Sunday Chinese school to organizing football matches for Chinese youngsters. Its counterpart in Liverpool is the Wah-Shing (Voice of China) Association which, like the Kung Ho, regularly shows films from Communist China.

The third party engaged in the "hearts and minds" battle in the Chinese community is the Hong Kong Government Office. The Office has a liaison department which gives advice and information to Chinese immigrants and groups on a range of matters. In the early days, when there were very few Chinese voluntary associations, the Office also used to assist Chinese workers in filling in forms and other applications.

Chinese Triads (Secret Societies)

Perhaps the least-known of Chinese societies are the Triads. The only time they appear in the public eye is when some of their members are caught drug-smuggling or charged with criminal acts of violence against fellow Chinese. It is true that the Triads worldwide are today involved in illicit activities of various sorts. In Britain, the Wo Shing Wo and "14 K" societies are engaged in drug-trafficking and running protection rackets which cover illegal gaming dens and Chinese restaurants. Some restaurant owners are paying as much as £300 per week in protection money. The "14 K" society was named after the number of the house in Po Wah Road, Canton, where the society was founded some sixty years ago.

However, the Triads' present control of vice is a far cry from their original aims. In Imperial China, the secret societies were the principal instruments for the expression of popular grievances. In their resistance to the state and its officialdom, the Triads often took up the cause of poverty-stricken peasants. More specifically, the Triads were established in 1674, in the reign of the Manchu Emperor, Kang Hsi, as a political force dedicated to overthrow the Manchus. In order to understand what they had against the Manchus, it is necessary to trace the Buddhist connections of their founding members. The story is as follows.

In the seventeenth century, a sect of Shao Lin Buddhist monks in Fujian province had been granted Imperial favour and honours for helping the Manchu Emperor to put down a rebellion. This state of well-being did not last long. Out of jealousy or spite, one of the monks reported to the Emperor that the Abbot was plotting against him. Troops were sent to the monastery and, despite brave resistance from the 128 monks trained in martial arts, only five survived the attack. The five survivors pledged to set up their own monasteries as centres of resistance against the Manchus.

The Triads trace their origins to these five

ancestors. The word "Triad" actually comes from the symbol "triangle", which, for the societies, represents Heaven, Earth and Man. Initiation into the society involves an elaborate ceremony designed to gain the initiate's total loyalty. The initiate is expected to renounce his own blood relatives and family and swear allegiance to his Triad "brothers". Incidentally, the penal code in China at this time held that brotherhoods formed outside the bond of kinship or marriage were punishable by death.

The Triads were closely involved in two of the greatest revolts of the nineteenth century: the Taiping uprising against the Manchu rulers and the Boxer (Fists of Righteous Harmony) rebellion against the foreign colonialists. After the overthrow of the Manchus and the establishment of a republic in 1911, the Triads gradually lost their roots with the poor, as they started backing those political leaders who promised the most power and wealth. This so happened to be the nationalist Kuomintang, which utilized the Triads as a private army to maintain order in the cities. With the Communist victory, large numbers of Triad members fled the mainland for Hong Kong, South East Asia and other overseas Chinese settlements in the West. (For further details see Sean O'Callaghan *The Triads: The Mafia of the Far East,* W.H. Allen & Co, 1981, p.9-42).

6

The Chinese Cultural Tradition

For nearly 5,000 years, China developed its own culture, largely in isolation of different cultural traditions of equal strength.

As China is one of the oldest agricultural civilizations in the world, much of Chinese culture, including the joyous festivals celebrated by the Chinese, is influenced by the historical necessity of coming to terms with nature. At the same time, strong kinship ties provided the basis for the earliest and most enduring social organizations in Chinese history. These ties extended not only to existing family members but also to a family's deceased ancestors.

The early development of kinship as a basis of social order gave rise to a moral philosophy, Confucianism, which today is part of the heritage of Chinese all over the world. The teachings of Confucius and his emphasis on the individual as a social being, with a set of moral duties, have had a lasting influence on various aspects of Chinese social and cultural life. In the old China, children were told tales based on the Confucian classics, scholars would debate the meaning of Confucian precepts, and a knowledge of Confucius's works was essential to pass the civil service examinations.

Despite the tremendous social change in China and Hong Kong over the last 100 years, the influence of Confucius is still very much part of the heritage of the Chinese. Its legacy is built into the culture and customs of the Chinese.

The Confucius In Us All

Up to the end of the nineteenth century, China could be truly called a Confucian civilization. Confucius was born 2,500 years ago (551 BC), in the province of Shandong. Although his father's family name was Ho, Confucius was known as Kung-Fu-Zi. In his youth, he worked as a junior official and was ambitious to attain high office. Since the highest positions in government at the time were reserved for members of the nobility, Confucius decided to establish himself as a teacher, to expound his views on society and government. Because of his reputation as a learned scholar, he became a consultant to different princely rulers and also attracted a large following of disciples.

Confucius taught and emphasized "love", "righteousness", "propriety" (observance of rules) and "wisdom", as a set of moral truths. For the individual, the primary task was to cultivate oneself as a true gentleman or sage (zun-zi). The superior man was one who had cultivated these cardinal virtues and was therefore able to rule over those who laboured with their hands. The goal for society was to achieve universal order and harmony, under the rule of a perfect sage-ruler.

For Confucius, there were five moral relationships (wu-lun) requiring the obedience and the fulfilling of obligations of those involved in them. These relationships were between ruler – minister (official), father – son, husband – wife, between brothers and between friends. The individual existed only in his relationship to others in these social positions, whether father, brother, friend or husband. Not surprisingly, the family and clan had a key role in achieving orderly relations between people in different social positions. Confucian family life was to instil a sense of respect for authority and, by so doing, ensure stability of the dynasty.

The link between the family and the state was

Rice harvesting. Many Chinese festivals have their roots in agriculture.

Lam's Ancestral Hall in Sha Tin, 1981.

clearly seen by Confucius. For the sage-philosopher, the virtue of filial piety (duties of children to elders) was of great importance to good government. Filial piety was not invented by Confucius. (The feudal rulers had organized their clan members into a hierarchy, in which each had a recognized status.) But he sought to uphold the existing order by stressing respectful obedience to parents and loyalty to one's rulers. The China of his day was rife with civil war and disorder, because of family disputes and the challenge of the rulers' authority by "disloyal" officials. So the first priority of a filial son is "propriety". A son must be obedient to his parents and accord them their due respect, even if they are "unjust" in their actions.

Political order, for Confucius, was not to be achieved by physical force or by following a legal set of rules. An enlightened ruler used moral force and example to gain the respect of his subjects. It is sometimes thought that Confucianism is a religion, in that the Emperor's claim to be ruler was conditional on his following the "way of Heaven" or "Heaven's Will" (*Tien Ming*). Tranquillity and social harmony in his Empire indicated Heaven's approval of his rule, whilst chaos reflected a morally degenerate leadership. Yet "Heaven" (*Shang Di*) was not an almighty creator nor God, but a set of eternal moral laws which regulated the universe (including human society). So the cultivation of the virtues of loyalty, filial piety and sincerity would ensure harmony and peace not only within the family but in society at large.

The Confucian Family

Chinese families expect their sons to remain dutiful all their life. Being "filial" (*xiao*) to one's parents is perhaps the most important duty for sons. This includes not only caring for elderly parents, in particular mothers, but also continuing to be dependent on and subordinate to one's father, as a lifelong obligation. Alfred Chan thought that the economic transformation and social changes in China and Hong Kong over the last few decades have made this Confucian ideal less relevant to many Chinese. The greater financial independence of young people finding jobs in the urban sector, the growing sense of individualism and greater confidence of youth have, to some degree, weakened the authority of elders.

Confucius believed that the lifelong submission of sons to their fathers, who, in turn, would act kindly and with consideration, would ensure harmony within the family. It would seem, therefore, that a son would never be able to establish his own independent life. Daughters, on the other hand, were married off into their husbands' families for a lifelong role of subordination to their husbands and mothers-in-law. The birth of a son is the cause of much celebration in the Chinese household. In some areas of China today, families still hang a lantern outside the house, decorated with the word "prosperity". Not only can the young parents now face old age with security but also, for the wife, she has proved herself as a mother and met expectations as a daughter-in-law. For the young husband, he at last graduates from being a mere son to someone who has added a new generation to the family line. In the old China and even in some Chinese households today, the position of a childless woman was unfortunate. The daughter-in-law's infertility was considered a breach of filial piety which made it legitimate for a husband to take a second wife. Alfred Chan said, however, that the situation was changing today in Hong Kong. Although daughters-in-law were expected to stay at home to have children and do the housework, in working-class families both husband and wife have to go out to work in order to survive.

Honouring Ancestors

At a very young age, Chinese children are taught a variety of terms for addressing older relatives respectfully. For example, a father's brothers are always known as *shu-shu* and never addressed by their first names. These status terms confirm the expected relationship of deference and filiality between younger and older relatives. Chinese parents often introduce acquaintances to their children as "auntie" or "uncle", implying that they should receive the same respect from the younger generation as an older relative would.

The Chinese do not pay respect only to living elders but also to their deceased ancestors. This form of respect has been termed "ancestor worship", although it does not have the same meaning as worshipping a God. Chinese customs include an enormous body of rituals designed to keep alive the good deeds and achievements of deceased ancestors.

At the same time, the actions of living relatives affect the reputation and well-being not only of living family members but also of the deceased. For the Chinese "sojourner" or migrant, therefore, his success was framed in terms of "bringing a good name and glory" to the whole ancestral clan. In traditional China, respect for the dead was best illustrated in the lavish expenditure on the funeral of a deceased father. Not only did this confirm the social status of the deceased, it also proved the filial piety of his children.

Villages in southern China tended to have an ancestral hall to commemorate ancestors on the father's side of the family. The Chan family's native village in Guangdong province had its own ancestral hall (*chi tong*). David Wan also recalled that his native village of Cheung Lek Mei in the New Territories had an ancestral hall in memory of all deceased relatives on his grandfather's side. The *chi tong* was in a state of disrepair today, as no one was left in the village to look after it.

The ancestral hall served as a mark of wealth for the kinship-village. In the ancestral hall, the ancestral tablet, which was a red scroll of paper or inscribed plaque containing the names of the deceased ancestors, served as the centre of ritual activities. Ancestors were worshipped on all major festivals, such as Lunar New Year, Ching Ming and Chung Yang. Worship in the ancestral hall was essentially a man's world. Only the most senior women would, on leaving this world, have their names listed in the ancestral tablet.

Ancestor worship is not openly practised by Britain's Chinese population. There are no ancestral halls in Chinatown, as most of the Chinese migrants still trace their line of descent to ancestors in Hong Kong's New Territories or southern China. It is possible, though, that some Chinese households in Britain have erected their own domestic altars to remember deceased relatives. To some extent, being in a "foreign" land has forced the Chinese to modify their customary burial practices. For example, some of the gravestones in the "Chinese cemeteries" in Liverpool have had inscriptions in both Chinese and English for the last 50-60 years. Presumably this was to enable cemetery employees and future generations of relatives who may not be able to read Chinese to identify the early migrants' graves.

Marriage: The First Stage in Extending the Family Line

Most Chinese families see their primary duty to their ancestors as maintaining the family line. In this sense, not having children would be the greatest breach of filial duty. Marriage, therefore, is the first step in continuing the ancestral line. In fact, a man who was unmarried on death would be buried without ceremony.

Alfred and Alice Chan were married in a British registry office in 1976. Three years later, they returned to Hong Kong to receive their parents' blessing and celebrate the event with their families. Alfred's marriage had not been arranged by his

Alfred and Alice Chan posing for their wedding photo in Hong Kong. Alice in traditional wedding dress. The Chans returned to Hong Kong in 1979 to celebrate their wedding in Britain with their relatives.

Alice Chan Lai Hing and her son Kwan Yu at home in Penicuik, Midlothian.

parents as was the case in traditional China. In urban Hong Kong today, more and more young people are choosing their own marriage partners, although this is still generally not the case in the villages.

Although Alfred and Alice were married in Britain, their parents, on their behalf, still practised some of the traditional rites of marriage laid down in the Confucian classic, *The Record of Rites*. These rites usually follow a set pattern. Arranged marriages are commonly initiated by a mother asking a matchmaker (*mei ren*), who would be a married female relative or friend, to make some enquiries in the families of eligible girls or boys. When a suitable match is found, the matchmaker then informs both families of the times and dates of birth of the boy and girl. This information would be written as eight characters and a professional soothsayer would be asked to interpret the compatibility of the match. The Chinese often say that marriages are "made in Heaven", although, in reality, the wishes of both sets of parents are primary. Essentially, the chief requisites for a daughter-in-law would be good physical health to ensure that she could bear children, diligence in doing housework, and a good reputation.

When the two families are satisfied with the match, a formal engagement ceremony is set. Either the boy's father or a senior male relative would visit the girl's family with gifts of perishable food such as cakes, fruits and roast pork or a suckling pig. In addition, he would take a dowry payment. In rural China today, this money is used to buy furniture for the couple's bridal suite in the husband's household. In addition, the boy's parents would present jewellery for their future daughter-in-law. Unusual, perhaps, is the fact that the future bride and groom do not have to be present at this engagement ceremony. Alfred and Alice were in Britain when their parents made all these arrangements. The betrothal is the first act of marriage, as, from this day onwards, the two families refer to each other as relatives.

After the engagement, a wedding day is fixed. In the old China, up to three years might elapse before the actual wedding took place. This enabled the bride's family to prepare the wedding garments, bedding and other clothes for their daughter's married life. On the wedding day, the groom's family would send a decorated sedan chair, carried by four able-bodied junior relatives. The traditional bridal robe was made out of red silk or satin, with a cotton-padding to symbolize fertility. Two of the bride's brothers or uncles would accompany her to

43

the groom's household. The journey on the sedan chair symbolized the physical removal and the transfer of the girl's loyalty to her in-laws. Even in modern China, brides are transported from one village to another on a bicycle, to symbolize this dramatic move.

On the bride's arrival at the groom's village and house, both bride and groom pay homage to the gods of Heaven and Earth. The bride then bows to the bridegroom's parents and makes offerings to their ancestors. After the formal ceremonies, the young couple enter the bridal chamber with younger relatives and friends, for merry-making. In the old China, this would often be the first time that the bride and bridegroom would see each other face to face.

There is a certain amount of sex inequality in these marriage arrangements. For instance, when a man's wife died, he was free to marry again. A number of the early seamen took a second wife in Britain with the consent of their parents who, as far as they were concerned, already had a daughter-in-law in the family. In the old days, a widow was not allowed to remarry, particularly if she already had children. If she did remarry, there would be no parade or ceremony marking this event and her new husband would treat her more like a maid than a wife.

Social Identity versus Free Expression

An understanding of the importance placed on "face" (reputation) would perhaps provide an insight into the so-called "inscrutability" of the oriental Chinese. The blank, expressionless face of the Chinese child in school or the sudden silence of a Chinese caller at the other end of the telephone have a rational explanation. In both cases, if the question asked would involve a loss of face, because the answer is not known, then the solution would be to keep quiet. To lose one's face is to lose one's human dignity. In Chinese terms, men are human because they have a face to protect.

From a young age, Chinese children are taught not to deviate or "stick out" from the proper modes of conduct in relating to elders, by shaming them whenever they do so. Family scandals are to be avoided at all costs, as this would involve the whole family losing face. Even in business arrangements, the fear of losing face would call for the services of a

mutually known intermediary, to find a face-saving agreement for both parties concerned. For example, if a house-owner wanted a builder to work a bit faster, he would ask a mutual friend to politely communicate this request, so as to avoid the possibility of being insulted. The builder, in turn, would probably oblige the mutual friend for fear of losing face in the friend's eyes if he did not.

The high value placed on being polite and obeying the rules, to avoid "losing face", accounts for the Chinese tendency to keep their emotions to themselves. Personal feelings and family problems are often hidden behind walls of polite social forms. From young, Chinese children are taught that emotions are dangerous, as they would threaten social harmony based on proper rules of behaviour. In the old China, children caught quarrelling with their brothers or friends would be given a thrashing. In the West, "sincerity" means the honest expression of one's inner feelings. To the traditional Chinese, it meant that the expression of hostility should never be released against an authoritative individual. Self-assertion is not tolerated in Chinese culture. Instead, emphasis is placed on *chi ku* (literally "eat bitterness") or swallowing one's anger.

Whereas "saving face" was understandable in a face-to-face society where social harmony was of primary importance, many modern Chinese such as Shing Tung Chow see it as a barrier to the cultivation of a true democratic tradition. According to Shing Tung: "Our tradition of Confucianism has made us complacent. We look inward and are not expressive. The English try to adapt equipment to make it better but we Chinese believe in self-cultivation. Instead of improving the tools, we try to improve ourselves." Shing Tung did think, however, that this Confucian tradition has at least enabled the Chinese to achieve a greater degree of self-control over their emotions so that they do not get depressed so easily and are more able to control their tempers.

All societies provide a possible release from tight social control. In traditional China, to escape from the conformist grip of Confucianism, many Chinese elected to live close to nature, as Taoist hermits (see next section). Others joined brotherhood societies which were non-hierarchical. Several of China's most famous medieval novels, such as *The Water Margin*, reveal a strong element of escapism in the concept of brotherly friendship.

Taoism: Chinese Naturalism

It is now customary to identify Confucianism, Taoism and Buddhism as the three great "religions" in China. Taoism is a mystical philosophy and way of life that persisted for well over 2,000 years in China. As a philosophy, Taoism stressed the doctrine of following nature. Its founder is said to be Li Tan, who was known as Lao Zi (Aged Master). Reputed to have reached the age of 200, he was a senior contemporary of Confucius. His whole philosophy involved a rejection of the Confucian emphasis on proper rites and moral propriety. In his masterly work, the *Tao Te Ching* (Classic of the Way and Power), Lao Zi taught "Get rid of the wise, discard the learned and the people will benefit a hundredfold." Lao Zi attempted to reveal the laws underlying the changes of things in the universe. By calmly regulating one's actions in conformity with the course of nature, one could then live in harmony with it.

To most ordinary Chinese, including many of the overseas Chinese in Britain, Taoism represents a set of magical beliefs and occult practices designed to *control* or *alter* the course of nature. In the past, many people believed that Taoist "priests", through a series of rituals and magical formulae and healing potions, could command unseen spirits to ensure a good harvest, avoid sickness in the family or even prolong life. In Hong Kong and parts of South East Asia today, Taoist priests are often called upon to officiate at funeral services, together with Buddhist monks.

Although worlds apart, Confucianism and Taoism were both expressions of the aspirations and inspirations of the Chinese farmer. Confucianism was the philosophy of everyday social life, with its complex social relationships. Taoism symbolized man's coming to terms with nature, as the provider of food and sustenance, and it emphasized man's human roots in nature.

The Taoist tradition is perhaps no more evident than in Chinese poetry and painting. For example, Chinese landscape and animal paintings can be traced back to Taoist roots. In the West, Taoism has become a popular philosophy for people seeking an "alternative" way of life.

Other Religious Traditions

The third religious influence on the Chinese people

Example of Chinese painting on rice paper using ground black ink and water. Chinese paintings are normally scrolled on a silk background. Animals, birds and insects are often favourite subjects.

was the spread of Buddhism from India. Buddhism was first introduced into China probably around the first half of the first century AD. It was the *Mahayana* (Large Vehicle) form of Buddhism that spread to China. As a learning (*fo xue*), it appealed to the educated, but Buddhism was popularized as a religion (*fo jiao*) for the common people. Unlike Tibet, Thailand and Cambodia, however, China never became a Buddhist country. In China, the existing influences of Confucianism, Taoist beliefs and ancestor worship modified the entering stream of Buddhist teachings.

In Britain, there are no Chinese Buddhist temples. The absence of a public place of worship, however, does not imply that the Chinese in Britain have abandoned all their religious beliefs. David Wan's mother, for example, is a Buddhist. When she returns to Hong Kong, she makes a point of paying homage to various Buddhist shrines such as that of Guan-Yin, the Goddess of Mercy and offspring of Amitabha (Buddha). David's grandmother in Hong Kong is still very religious. During all the major Chinese festivals she would pay respects to a variety of Buddhist deities and benevolent spirits.

There is a pragmatic streak in Chinese religious beliefs. Inevitably, the purpose of visiting these spirit-deities is to ask them for "luck", in order to achieve a long life, good health, material success and a large family. But the Hong Kong Chinese are probably more superstitious than their counterparts in mainland China today. Shing Tung Chow's family, for example, are all atheists. Shing Tung was quite scathing of Chinese religious worship. "The Chinese basically are not religious. We are superstitious as a country. We believe any rubbish but we never formed a religion." Even Shing Tung's grandmother, after living under Communist Chinese rule for 15 years, has discarded most of her superstitious beliefs.

Despite the early presence of Jesuit priests in China, Christianity only began to spread after the opening up of the treaty ports of Canton, Shanghai and Amoy to European traders in the nineteenth century. It is difficult to estimate the number of Chinese Christians living in Britain. One thing for sure, though, is that the majority of Christians from Hong Kong belong to the Protestant faith.

In Liverpool, the Chinese Gospel Church is probably one of the oldest Chinese Christian churches in Britain. In London, the Anglican church in St Martin-in-the-Fields has had a Chinese priest for the last 20 years already. There is also a Chinese Rhenish church in West London. In almost every British city where the Chinese have settled, Chinese Christian associations have been established. In London, the Chinese Overseas Christian Mission acts as an umbrella organization for all the Chinese Protestant groups in Europe.

Many of Edinburgh's Chinese are Christians. Alfred Chan has observed that the majority of

Victor Lye Pak Fun and family at the baptism of their baby, Jeremy, in a Catholic church in Kenton, Middlesex. Godparents on right.

The animals of the Chinese Zodiac: the rat, the ox, the tiger, the hare, the dragon, the snake, the horse, the goat, the monkey, the cock, the dog, the pig.

Edinburgh Chinese from the Hong Kong island of Ap Chau belong to the "True Jesus Church". Alfred also thought that the strength of Christian beliefs in Edinburgh has made the local Chinese population less enthusiastic about gambling.

Generally speaking, church services are attended by both elderly and young Chinese. In many cases, the church would also run a number of social activities for Chinese families and youngsters. Many of the part-time Chinese mother-tongue classes in Britain were, in fact, initiated by Chinese Christian organizations.

Christianity has not only made an impact in urban Hong Kong; the missionary influence is also strong in remoter parts of the territory. It is not uncommon, therefore, to see small villages with their own church. A number of villagers, however, have joined the church either to take advantage of the welfare benefits available from missionary relief organizations or to make use of better educational opportunities existing in the missionary schools.

Chinese Festivals

In agrarian societies like China, Thailand and Vietnam, the cultural festivals can be traced back to the need to thank the "gods" and "benevolent spirits" for providing a good harvest. The celebration of festivals also serves as a reward for farmers, who live a life of toil throughout the year.

The ancient lunar calendar is used to set the dates of traditional Chinese festivals. In Britain, only Lunar New Year is publicly celebrated by the overseas Chinese. As we shall see, other major festivals such as Mid-Autumn festival may be celebrated privately within a Chinese family.

But, first, a description of the Chinese lunar calendar is needed to explain why the same festival never falls on the same date when translated into the Western calendar. For several thousand years, China has used the lunar calendar. The year is divided into twelve months of either 29 or 30 days. Every 3 years but sometimes 2, the calendar is further adjusted by the addition of an extra month. Each month has two

One of the Metropolitan Police's few Chinese constables on duty in Soho during Chinese New Year, 1983.

Re-living China's past: some of the folk opera performers of Camden Chinese Community Centre in an off-stage pose during Chinese New Year, 1983.

seasonal changes or periods, named after the particular weather conditions and type of farming job done in each period. This system of categorization enabled farmers to plan their schedule of work. Each year is designated by one of twelve symbolic animals which repeat in a twelve-year cycle. There is a story as to how the naming of years after animals arose. According to legend, the Emperor of Heaven summoned all the animals of the world to appear before him and promised that anyone who paid him homage would have a year named after him. Only twelve animals made the journey, led by the rat, with the pig coming in last place.

These symbolic animals also form the basis of the Chinese horoscope. The Chinese believe that all people born under the same animal-sign have certain attributes in common. Each animal-sign is associated with a range of positive and negative qualities. The "Dragon" is a very popular animal-sign for the Chinese. Like the tiger, dragons are believed to have the potential to be rulers. In Hong Kong and South East Asia, it is common for young married couples to plan to have children in certain years designated by auspicious animal-signs.

Lunar New Year [Chinese Spring Festival]

New Year is the most widely celebrated Chinese festival amongst Chinese communities world-wide. In China, New Year is called Spring Festival, representing a new agricultural cycle. Chinese New Year 1984 (Year of the Rat) fell on 2 February, on the Western calendar. Traditionally, celebrations would last fifteen days. In Hong Kong all employees are given three days off for the festivities, whilst the schools close for a whole week. By contrast, the

49

celebrations for Chinese New Year in Britain are combined into one day: normally the first Sunday of the New Year.

In Soho, the annual New Year celebrations are organized by the Chinatown Chinese Association. Every year the association raises money for the street decorations and the programme of celebration involving three lion-dance teams and a song performance. In the tradition of mutual help, the Chinese businesses in Soho all contribute to the cost of the celebrations. A red packet containing money (*lai see*) is hung out of the windows of the restaurants and shops, together with a head of lettuce or cabbage for the dancing lions to collect.

The Wan family always celebrate Chinese New Year in Britain. David and his parents normally would make a point of watching the lion-dance performances in Soho. When they were still in Hong Kong, David's parents and grandparents would celebrate all the major festivals in the Chinese calendar. Alfred Chan's family in Hong Kong also celebrate all the major festivals. Shing Tung Chow and his family do not celebrate New Year in a big way. He pointed out that unless they worked in Soho Chinatown, most Chinese would not bother attending the public celebrations. Furthermore, most Chinese restaurants are open all day on New Year's Day.

In Hong Kong, preparations for New Year begin on the 20th day of the twelfth moon (month). All houses are swept and cleaned in preparation for a great family reunion, including the living and the dead. On the 23rd day, offerings are made to the "Kitchen-God", who sets off to report the conduct of the family to the ruler of Heaven. One of the dishes offered to him is a sweet of sticky rice, either to "sweeten" his report or to seal his mouth from making bad utterances. These preparations are still followed by the Wans in London.

Most families would stay up on New Year's Eve to welcome the New Year in. The first activity on New Year's Day is to pay homage to ancestors. Incense sticks are lit and all male members of the family bow in front of the ancestral table. When the ceremony is over, the gaiety begins. Children and junior members of the family are given *lai see* for good luck. Fire-crackers are let off and red posters are hung, carrying messages of celebration. Traditionally, fire-crackers were ignited to ward off demon spirits.

Visits to relatives and close friends take place on the first and second days. The Wans in London also follow this custom, but they make a point of having a family dinner on New Year's Day. New clothes are worn when visiting relatives, to signify the discarding of the old year.

During the New Year period, festive food is served, including melon seeds, preserved fruits, sweets and fried cakes such as *jian dui* made from peanuts, sesame and molasses. For the Chinese, the basic sense of well-being and security remains linked throughout life to the ritual of eating. Much attention is paid to the art of eating and different kinds of food are prepared for each festival.

The third day is known as "Squabble Day". No visiting is done on this day to avoid any quarrels or arguments which would be bound to arise. On the 15th day, a three-day lantern festival begins, to mark the end of the New Year celebrations. In the old China, left-over food would be consumed, although in Hong Kong, special dumplings would be served. Alfred Chan thought that this lantern festival (*ling xiu*) reinforced the patriarchal nature of Chinese society. Those families in Hong Kong with male descendants would hang lanterns in their homes to symbolize their good luck and prestige.

Ching Ming [Festival of Bright and Clear]

This is a ten-day festival starting on the 19th day of the second month. Originally, the festival meaning "clear and bright" was to celebrate the weather and the temporary dominance of *Yang* (light) over *Yin* (darkness). The custom of *sao mu*, or sweeping and cleaning the graves, has become associated with this period. In Hong Kong, the graves of ancestors are visited and ritual offerings of food made. Sometimes, paper images of houses and carriages are burnt, to pass on as smoke in the "invisible world". In London and Liverpool, Ching Ming is celebrated only by those families who have relatives buried in the local cemeteries there.

Mid-Autumn Moon Festival

Celebrated on the 15th day of the eighth month, this was one of the most joyous occasions of the year in the old China, as the harvest was assured. The moon is at its brightest and fullest on this day. In modern times, it has become a day of thanksgiving and happy

The possible development of the Chinese character for "fish".

family reunion. Mooncakes with centres made out of sweet pastes or sweetmeats are sold in Soho Chinatown. Some Chinese associations, such as the Chinese Midlands Association, organize an evening get-together for members. The cakes have a special significance, recalling the uprising against the Mongol invaders in the fourteenth century. Messages for the Chinese troops were secretly passed on inside the mooncakes.

Language as a Cultural Vehicle

Chinese is the world's oldest language and has been in continuous use for 3,500 years. The written Chinese script is made up of characters or ideograms. The earliest markings that can be identified as Chinese writing were inscriptions scratched on tortoise shells and animal bones for the purposes of making predictions about the future.

Today, there are perhaps as many as 40,000 Chinese characters, although most people only use 3-4,000 in everyday life. Each character conveys not only the pronunciation but also ideas and objects in the form of picture symbols. In China, the art of character writing or calligraphy is appreciated as much as Chinese painting.

Although a variety of dialects are spoken, they all share the same written language. The character for "culture", pronounced "wen" in Mandarin, is pronounced "man" in Cantonese; but the meaning of the character, when written, is clear to all dialect speakers. Mandarin is the official language spoken in the People's Republic of China and Taiwan. Cantonese is the lingua franca of Hong Kong.

The Chinese language is not only a vital unifying factor. It also serves as a vehicle for preserving the cultural heritage of a people, as it is passed on from one generation to another. By learning their mother-tongue, Chinese children are socialized into the culture of their forefathers.

In Britain, the Chinese community has perhaps nowhere shown more unity of purpose and firm conviction than in the issue of Chinese-language teaching. For most parents, teaching the mother-tongue to their children is one way of preventing a breakdown in parent-child relationships. It is also considered the duty of the young to accept and appreciate their ancestral culture. A person who has *wang ben* (forgotten his origins) is considered most unfilial. In the late 1960s and 1970s, a number of Chinese parents sent their children back to Hong Kong for periods lasting several years. The idea was to socialize the child in a Chinese Confucian environment, where he would not only learn Chinese but also internalize the moral values inherent in his ancestral culture. In most cases, the child was brought up by the grandparents who remained in Hong Kong.

Chinese parents encourage their British-born children to attend mother-tongue classes. David Wan's thirteen-year-old sister Angela, who was born in Britain, attends week-end Chinese-language classes organized by a Chinese voluntary association in Tower Hamlets. When she was eight, she was sent back to Hong Kong for two years to learn Chinese properly. Angela's mother accompanied her home but, according to David, his young sister had great difficulty understanding the teacher.

The first Chinese school in Britain was established as early as 1935, in Pennyfields in London's East End. Known as the Zhong-hua Middle School, it had fewer than 30 Chinese children attending classes. At present, there are around 70 Chinese-language classes or supplementary schools operating all over the country. Most of them are run by Christian Chinese organizations and community associations.

Classes are generally held on Saturdays and Sundays, although some of the "schools" also hold classes during the week. In the majority of cases, the Hong Kong Government Office in London provides text books for these classes and, sometimes, a small grant for running expenses.

The Chinese Chamber of Commerce Chinese School in Frith Street, Soho, is the largest school of its kind in Europe. Over 900 pupils are enrolled today, most of them in primary-level classes. The school was first opened in 1968 with 20 pupils. The school is well-equipped with a library and is run by seven fully-qualified Chinese teachers. Classes go on all day at week-ends and from 5 to 7 pm on weekdays. Money to pay for the renovation of the premises in Frith Street was raised through donations and contributions from the Chinese community in Europe and from Hong Kong. A weekly subsidy is provided by the Hong Kong Government Office and all pupils are charged a fee of £15, for a year's tuition. Cantonese is taught at primary-level, and Mandarin is offered for senior students. The school also offers classes in calligraphy and Chinese painting, and sponsors poetry recitals and song contests.

Compared with this school, most of the other mother-tongue supplementary schools lack finances, have inadequate premises and lack training facilities for teachers who are, in most cases, university students or unqualified volunteers.

Chinese Names

So far, readers will note that all the young Wans, Chows and Chans mentioned in this book have Christian and Chinese first names. Surprisingly, perhaps, many of the younger Chinese from Hong Kong and South East Asia have Christian names, even though they may not be Christians. Both Alfred Chan and Shing Tung Chow agreed that "English" names were fashionable in Hong Kong, as they were a symbol of "being modern" or keeping up with the times. Shing Tung thought that it was a deliberate policy of the education authorities in Hong Kong to encourage pupils, even those attending Chinese secondary schools, to adopt Christian names, such as John, Paul, Mary or Teresa.

Chinese names, although funny-sounding to outsiders, do follow a meaningful pattern. The surname or family name always comes first and there are fewer than 500 surnames in use. In the West, some Chinese have placed their surname at the end, as in European names, so as to avoid difficulties and misunderstandings with the education and immigration authorities.

Since there are only a limited number of Chinese surnames, a person can therefore be more uniquely identified by his or her "first" names, which follow the family name. Single-character first names usually depict a characteristic or noble value which the parents wish the child to have. Boys are often referred to as sincere, brave or clever. Girls would have names designating them as virtuous or beautiful or be named after certain flowers such as lotus, orchid and chrysanthemum.

In double-character first names, the first character usually describes the generational rank of the offspring. All the sons in the Chow family have the generational character "Shing", whilst the Chan family sons have the generational character "Cheong". Similarly, the generational characters of Shing Tung's and Alfred's sons are "Fan" and "Kwan" respectively. Alfred's sisters all have the generational character "Sun" as part of their first names.

When the generational character is put together with another character, Chinese first names then depict certain characteristics or values as in single-character names. Alfred Chan's first name is "Cheong Ming", which, put together, means "reknown intellectual". Alice Chan's first name is "Lai Hing", meaning "beautiful maiden". Their son's name "Kwan Yu" means "integrity and honesty". In the Chow family, "Shing Tung", when placed together, means "Success in the East". Shing Tung's mother is called "Man Wun" ("cultural diffusion"), his wife, "Miu Heng", is "virtuous and lovely", and his son, "Fan Zheng", is supposed to be "glorious in politics".

7

Close Ties
with a Distant Home

Many of the first-generation migrants who came to Britain after the Second World War still maintain close ties with their home villages and relatives in Hong Kong. Such contact takes the form of correspondence, the occasional overseas trunk call or visit home, and the regular remittance of money to relatives. The Hong Kong Chinese newspapers also help the Chinese in Britain and their relations back home to keep informed of one another. Newspapers such as *Sing Tao Daily* (European edition) normally reserve a page to report the activities of Chinese workers in Britain. News from Hong Kong and the New Territories is also given prominence.

Remittances

The Chinese from Hong Kong have certainly not forgotten their family and relatives whom they left behind. In the 1950s and 1960s, a Chinese worker would send between 20-40 per cent of his income back to his relatives. These remittances went not only to immediate family members but also to finance communal projects for the whole village. Annual remittances in the 1970s fluctuated between HK$50-100 million. Since then, of course, the wives, children and other dependants of Chinese workers arrived in Britain in increasing numbers.

One would expect the flow of remittances to decrease with the reunion of families in Britain. None of the three families introduced in this book sends regular remittances back to Hong Kong. Shing Tung Chow's grandparents (father's side) and three uncles still live in Hong Kong. However, they are comfortably-off and so do not require any financial help. The Wan family have no immediate relatives remaining in the New Territories and so do not send

any money home. In fact, their ancestral village, Cheung Lek Mei, is no longer inhabited, as all the families have either migrated overseas or moved to the town of Sha Tin. Alfred Chan cannot afford to send regular remittances to his parents who have retired. However, they are being looked after by Alfred's brothers in Hong Kong. As an act of filial piety, Alfred would remit a small sum of money on his parents' birthdays and at Chinese New Year.

Remittances have totally transformed the migrants' home villages. Of the 600 villages in the New Territories, around 40 or 50 are dependent on regular remittances for up to 50 per cent of their income. These emigrant villages are inhabited primarily by elderly relatives and young dependants and wives who have not joined their husbands abroad. Living standards are on the whole far higher than those enjoyed by urban workers and other villages in the New Territories.

Bereft of their male workers, these emigrant villages have turned into rural pockets of lavish consumption, as they no longer produce anything of economic value. The explosion in the property market a decade ago also provided windfall earnings for some of the villagers, who sold their land to the government or to urban developers.

As mentioned earlier, the flow of money back home did not only take the form of remittances to relatives. Migrants from the New Territories also contributed to the upkeep and construction of communal buildings such as the village ancestral hall. These contribution drives were an integral part of peasant life in southern China, where every temple or hall was built with money donated by kinsmen at home and abroad. Representatives of the

Sha Tin, 1983.

Liu clan in the New Territories, for example, came to Britain in 1971 to raise funds for a secondary school. Over HK$350,000 was raised from clan members in Britain, Holland and Belgium alone.

Other Ties to Homeland

Regular visits home are another way in which close ties are maintained between Chinese workers and their relatives in Hong Kong. Chinese New Year seems to be the most popular time to make a home visit. During this time, all the flights to Hong Kong are well-booked in advance and special flights are chartered by one of the Chinese travel agencies in London.

Alfred and Alice Chan have been back twice, in 1978 and 1983, since coming to Britain. Although David Wan's most recent visit to Hong Kong was in 1979, his parents take turns to go back to Hong Kong every year. As they have to keep their take-away open, Mr and Mrs Wan are not able to make the home visit together. In some cases, important family matters are not decided until the migrant workers come home. Generally, however, these home visits are purely social, although younger workers may return to Hong Kong to seek prospective marriage partners.

Until recently, these visits were an opportunity for the returning migrants to display their newly-acquired wealth, by giving presents or holding elaborate banquets. For those Chinese migrants who still see their native villages as their home, these lavish displays serve to reinforce their status in and commitment to the New Territories communities.

Another indication of the strong ties with the homeland is the frequency of phone calls made to Hong Kong. Mr and Mrs Wan would normally ring their relatives in Hong Kong on Chinese New Year.

A new bungalow in the New Territories, built with money remitted by a restaurant worker in Britain.

However, other Chinese in Britain make more frequent calls home. Until the closure of its telephone service in 1981, the 24-hour post office in Trafalgar Square, near to Soho, used to take over 10,000 calls a month to Hong Kong.

As time goes on, these ties with the home villages and relatives in Hong Kong are bound to weaken. The reunion of wives and children with Chinese workers in Britain has certainly affected the flow of remittances. Uncertainty over the future of Hong Kong, with the coming expiry of the New Territories lease in 1997, has also made some Chinese families re-think their plans of returning to Hong Kong. Leaving politics aside, having established themselves in Britain, many Chinese are beginning to think of settling down in their newly adopted country.

Hong Kong: Past and Future
A new dilemma faces those Chinese who may be planning to return to Hong Kong one day. The search for better job prospects was certainly one factor which led to the arrival of Chinese migrants in

Britain. But also, for nationalistic-minded Chinese like Alfred Chan and Shing Tung Chow, the lack of democracy in Hong Kong made the idea of a career in the territory less attractive. In Alfred's own words, the Hong Kong education system served to deter students from becoming politically aware. "The whole education system tries to deter students from politics including humanity subjects. History is grossly inadequate, particularly modern Chinese history." According to Alfred, European history is a compulsory subject up to Form 3 secondary level. Even modern Chinese history is biased in favour of the British point of view. The "Opium War" which ceded Hong Kong to Britain is, for example, referred to as the "Anglo-Chinese War", so as to paint the picture of a conflict between equals.

Both Alfred and Shing Tung subscribe to a view of Hong Kong's history which is more favourable to China. Such an interpretation would be as follows. Britain seized Hong Kong from China in three stages in the last century, after a long series of attempts at establishing trade with China. By the eighteenth century, the East India Company had managed to establish a foothold in Canton. Attempts to expand trade to other ports were unsuccessful, as successive Manchu Emperors restricted trade with the West to

Canton. British traders' sole export to China at this time was opium grown in India. As this opium was paid for in silver, the trade became a severe drain on the Chinese Treasury. In 1839, Lin Zexiu arrived in Canton with an Imperial mandate to suppress the opium trade. Britain's refusal to close down the opium trade led to the first Opium War (1840-2). The British victory was rewarded with the ceding of the island of Hong Kong in perpetuity, to Britain. Under the Treaty of Nanking (1842), Shanghai, Swatow, Ningpo, Amoy and Foochow were opened up as treaty ports, exempt from Chinese law and taxation.

For some time already, British merchants had been seeking an island enclave outside Chinese control. Hong Kong's early trade was primarily based on opium. Profits were phenomenal, with the exports of opium paying for imports of tea and silk from China. By the 1850s British traders demanded further concessions such as the right to manufacture in China. Gunboat diplomacy was used again to achieve this end. In 1860, the territory of Hong Kong was extended to include Kowloon Peninsula and Stonecutters Island. These extensions were conceded after Lord Elgin had led an invasion force into Peking, looting the Forbidden City and setting fire to the Summer Palace. Later in 1898, the Convention of Peking ceded an additional 365½ square miles in Sun On county, Guangdong province, on a 99-year lease to Britain. With the collapse of initial resistance from Chinese peasants in Sun On county, this area, now known as the New Territories, became an integral part of Hong Kong.

Hong Kong's population really started to increase from the 1930s, as Chinese refugees, fleeing from the Japanese advance and disruptions of the civil war, poured into the territory. Since the Communist victory on the mainland in 1949, over one million refugees and immigrants found a new home in Hong Kong. However, the majority of Hong Kong's 5.4 million inhabitants today were born in the territory.

From the 1840s to 1950s, apart from the Japanese occupation during 1942-5, Hong Kong served as a staging port and transhipment centre for trade between China and the West. With the Korean War and the U.N. embargo on the export of "strategic goods" to China, most of this trade was cut off. Hong Kong, therefore, turned to manufacturing and also established itself as a major financial centre.

With the expiry of the New Territories lease in 1997, most of Hong Kong's land area is scheduled to revert to China. This threatens the whole of Hong Kong, since the New Territories is the only area for industrial and residential expansion. Financiers and wealthy local businessmen, worried about the loss of confidence in Hong Kong's economy, had hoped that some form of British rule would continue after 1997.

Britain has now recognized China's sovereignty over Hong Kong. It also accepts that it will no longer rule the territory after 1997. China has assured Hong Kong that a future administration would have considerable local autonomy, with local Chinese running the place. Shing Tung Chow feels strongly over the issue of self-rule. He has set up a pressure group, the 1997 Action Group, which supports most of China's proposals. According to Shing Tung, "Every Chinese person would, if they were honest, find this an honourable solution."

Hong Kong's political system is a colonial one, which leaves little room for democracy. All the members of the Executive and Legislative Councils, the two main policy advisory bodies, are either appointed or ex-officio members, such as the Governor and Colonial Secretary. Most of the Chinese members appointed are prominent bankers and businessmen.

Shing Tung feels that the ordinary working people of Hong Kong should have a say in their future, as it is they who have to live under any solution worked out on their behalf. But is not "democracy" alien to the Chinese, seeing that the Confucian tradition stressed respect of superiors and obedience to the ruler? Shing Tung thought that Hong Kong had already adopted many Western institutions. Yet democracy, one of the "best traditions of the West", is not available to the population. After 150 years of colonialism, Hong Kong Chinese, according to Shing Tung, lacked confidence in themselves.

Many young nationalist Chinese see Hong Kong's prosperity as the result of the sweat and initiative of its working people and industrialists, as opposed to the orderly workings of the British administration. But has this prosperity benefited the majority? Over 60 per cent of Hong Kong's inhabitants live in subsidized public housing and hillside shanty huts. Yet, Hong Kong has more Rolls Royces and Mercedes per square mile than anywhere else in the

Jeans factory, Hong Kong, 1981.

world.

Shing Tung Chow was brought up in a two-bedroom apartment for eight people, in the working-class district of Kwun Tong. As a child, he shared one room with his sister, brothers and grandmother. Alfred Chan's apartment in Hong Kong was even more cramped, being one of the earlier resettlement blocks built by the government. All nine members of the Chan family had to make do with a common living area of 180 square feet. Alfred recalled how he had to do his homework whilst the TV set was on full blast and his younger sisters were jumping about all over the place.

Complaints about the condition of housing are rare, since people are glad to have a roof over their heads. There are 150,000 people on the housing waiting-list and a further 600,000 living in shanty-huts.

The old and the new. On the left and right are the older first phase public housing in Hong Kong. A family of 7-8 members would have to live in a common living space of 150 square feet.

8

Cousins from Vietnam

The most recent arrival of Chinese to Britain are the Chinese refugees from Vietnam. Since the Communist victory in Vietnam and the subsequent unification of the country in 1975, over 16,000 Vietnamese refugees have been resettled in Britain. As many as 70 per cent of them are ethnic Chinese, mainly from North Vietnam, which has been under Communist rule for 30 years. Most of those who arrived in Britain came from reception camps in Hong Kong which, at one time, provided temporary shelter for as many as 90,000 "boat people". Their arrival in Britain served to highlight existing problems facing the established Chinese community here.

Reasons for Exodus

Racial persecution certainly accounts for the flight of the minority Chinese from Vietnam. Relations between Vietnam and China deteriorated dramatically in 1977, as a result of Vietnam's increasing dependence on the Soviet Union and China's tilt towards the United States. As relations worsened, the Hanoi regime sought to represent its ethnic Chinese population as insidious agents of Peking. The Chinese were banned from a number of occupations, whilst their work permits and ration cards were withdrawn and their schools closed down. Hanoi's decision in the spring of 1978 to abolish private trade particularly affected the Chinese in the south. Private trade in Saigon, for example, was largely in the hands of the Chinese and many were forced out of business as a result of stringent economic measures introduced to control the retail sector.

Cultural differences were not a factor in the conflict. China and Vietnam share a common history and culture based on Confucianism, dating back 2,000 years. It is true, of course, that the Vietnamese are fiercely nationalistic, having made several attempts to reverse the Chinese occupation of their land which lasted nearly one thousand years. Yet before the start of the anti-Chinese policies in 1977, relations between the indigenous Vietnamese and minority Chinese gave little cause for concern. In fact, the Chinese were well-integrated in the political and economic life of North Vietnam. Refugees resettled in Britain have put the blame on the Vietnamese authorities for inciting racial hatred.

A Vietnamese reception centre in Tuen Mun, New Territories, Hong Kong. The centre was previously a multi-storey car park and factory complex.

A Vietnamese child at a Save The Children Fund reception centre. Young refugees were taught to use Western-style cutlery. They would have been used to chopsticks before.

The Reception Programme

On arrival in Britain, the refugees spent between three months and one year in reception centres, where they learnt about the British way of life and were prepared for resettlement. Three voluntary agencies, the British Refugee Council, Refugee Action [Save The Children Fund] and the Ockenden Venture, were given the task of receiving and resettling the refugees. Today, all but a handful of refugees have been resettled. At one time, though, there were as many as 40 reception centres all over the country. At the centres, the staff of the agencies would familiarize themselves with the needs of each family, the employment prospects of its members and its ties with other families already housed. Whilst at the centre, both the adults and young refugee children were given intensive tuition in the English language.

Resettlement

The resettlement programme followed a policy of dispersing the refugees in groups of 4–10 families to small towns or within a given housing authority area. Politically, this was designed to avoid any overt hostility from the local community to the presence of a large number of Vietnamese. The lack of housing, anyway, meant that no one authority could offer accommodation to a large number of families. Moreover, with the reduction of sympathetic media coverage of the refugees' plight, there soon followed

a dramatic reduction in the availability of housing. So desperate was the situation that offers of "unsuitable" and "sub-standard" housing were accepted, for fear of finding none whatsoever.

Educational Disadvantage

Because of their inadequate grasp of English, many refugee children, on entering school, were placed in remedial classes. Coming from an alien background, many Chinese and ethnic Vietnamese children found the learning experience in British classrooms quite different from their own back home, which stressed a Confucian respect for the authority of teachers.

Many adult refugees also felt that the language induction period was far too short and that they therefore left the reception centres ill-equipped to cope with their new environment. Inadequate resources and teaching facilities did not help matters. Another problem was the lack of understanding on the part of English-language teachers of the difficulties which native Chinese and Vietnamese speakers faced when learning English. Those refugees from a rural background also suffered the disadvantage of only having had a few years' primary school education. Emotionally, perhaps, many refugees were not in the right frame of mind to master a new language. The trauma of the refugee experience and anxieties about relatives still in

A chemistry class at the Save The Children Fund's Bingley School. No interpreters were allowed in the classroom. "This put extra pressure on the students but produced good results."

Vietnam occupied the minds of many adult refugees.

As with the newcomers from Hong Kong, it was the 14-16 year-old refugee children who faced the greatest difficulty in coping at school. For many of them, the one or two years in secondary school in Britain proved too short a time to equip them with the necessary qualifications for the world of work. Some attempts had been made to tackle this problem. In September 1980, the Save The Children Fund set up an experimental school for children from Vietnam who showed academic potential. These children attended a two-year course leading to GCE "O" levels and CSEs.

In the main, though, most teenagers from Vietnam leave school with no qualifications and unable to communicate in English. Alfred Chan pointed out, however, that some education institutions have tried to tackle this problem. Stevenson College in Edinburgh, for example, recently introduced a pre-vocational course for Vietnamese and Chinese teenagers, with intensive coaching in English language. A number of Hong Kong Chinese teenagers from restaurant backgrounds were also attending this course.

Employment Prospects

For most Vietnamese and Chinese refugees, the world of unemployment was what awaited them once resettled. The unemployment rate is said to be as high as 80 per cent amongst the refugee families from Vietnam. Those lucky enough to find work did not go through the Job Centres, which required job applicants to have a basic command of English. Many found work through direct contact with sympathetic employers or through the efforts of staff at the refugee agencies.

Job-finding was particularly difficult, given the deepening recession in Britain. Furthermore, most refugees were in occupations which were not easily employable in this country. Many were fishermen and farmers. Others were craftsmen and skilled workers, such as silversmiths, jewellery-makers, electricians, welders and even tram-repairers. There were also traders, hawkers and those in the professions such as doctors, dentists, lawyers and teachers.

Not surprisingly, those who found work were in unskilled jobs, such as hospital auxiliaries, store-keepers and night-watchmen. A number also found work in the bakeries. According to Alfred Chan, 40 refugee families had been resettled in Edinburgh, all of them ethnic Chinese. A number of them had been lucky enough to find work as chambermaids and kitchen assistants in hotels.

Unlike the Vietnamese refugees resettled in the USA or even the Hong Kong Chinese in Britain, many lack the necessary capital and confidence to set up their own businesses. This situation may be changing, however, as recently a number of refugees from Vietnam have set up their own take-aways and clothing workshops in the Midlands.

Social Isolation and Racial Harassment

The policy of dispersing refugees has served to increase the social isolation of families from Vietnam. Bleak employment prospects have also contributed to marital breakdowns, as the older men facing a lifetime of unemployment or "premature retirement" resort to alcohol. Acute depression and insecurity amongst the young have resulted in a number of teenage suicides and attempted suicides.

Youth delinquency is also on the increase, particularly amongst those from South Vietnam. The boredom generated by their unemployment has resulted in many younger refugees gravitating to the big cities such as London. For many, Soho Chinatown is their only focus of identity, reminding them of their home environment in Saigon (Ho Chi Minh city today).

Vietnamese and Chinese families have also become targets of racial abuse and attacks, both in the small towns and in the inner-city areas where they have been settled. In 1982, the horrendous persecution of Vietnamese and Chinese families in the Pepys Housing Estate, Lewisham, was exposed (*Daily Mail*, 12 March 1982). Members of the 36 refugee families on the estate were subjected to daily beatings and abuse from white residents. One Chinese mother also had her hair set on fire. These attacks forced the refugee families into further isolation, many not daring to wander out of their flats.

Those refugees living in small towns also face enormous pressures to assimilate; so much so that some of them have discarded their cultural identity and changed their name so as to be accepted by the host community.

Mutual Help and Self-Reliance

Right from the start, the Vietnamese and Chinese refugees, in fleeing from Vietnam, were at the mercy of the seas and dependent on the efforts of international officials and agency workers. This dependence on others has dampened any sense of self-reliance that they may have had. Moreover, those dispersed in small numbers to provincial towns do not have the confidence of numbers to provide mutual support for each other. This sense of social isolation partly accounts for why so many refugee families have, of their own accord, moved to large cities such as Birmingham and London, which have sizeable numbers of refugees from Vietnam.

Recently, attempts to mobilize Chinese and Vietnamese refugees have been made by members of their own ethnic group. Alfred Chan was originally involved in helping to set up a welfare project for Tower Hamlets' Chinese community. Over 70 Vietnamese families of Chinese descent arrived in the East End borough in 1981. The presence of refugee children still not acquainted with their new environment, coupled with the growing aspirations of Chinese teenagers already living in the borough, created a range of problems and special needs.

The Chinese Welfare Project currently runs weekly mother-tongue classes for children and teenagers, from both Hong Kong and Vietnam. Vietnamese Chinese children tend to have a lower grasp of Chinese than their peers from Hong Kong. Outings are also organized for teenagers, including to museums and the seaside. A youth club has been set up for Chinese teenagers to socialize and play badminton. Efforts are also being made by the Project's Chinese organizers to encourage unemployed school-leavers to join further education courses rather than sitting at home.

As elsewhere, the majority of the Tower Hamlets refugees are unemployed. A number of Chinese women do piecework sewing at home, for certain clothing firms. The refugee families have also set up their own co-operative, providing a mobile catering service and other commercial services.

The hopes, anxieties and aspirations of the Vietnamese are perhaps best illustrated by the experience of the Xian family, who are known to Alfred Chan. Mr Xian, a fisherman, left Haiphong in North Vietnam in 1979. His whole family of fourteen members are housed today in three council flats in the Isle of Dogs and Limehouse area. So far, only one of the three grown-up sons has found work. Mr Xian, who does not expect to find a job, lives in the hope that his younger children will go to college and make a better life for themselves.

Relations with the Hong Kong Chinese

The reaction of the Hong Kong Chinese to the arrival of their Vietnamese "cousins" has been somewhat mixed. In Tower Hamlets, the children from Hong Kong and Vietnam appear to get on well together. Moreover, most of the Chinese from Vietnam whom the author has met see themselves as overseas Chinese. Yet a number of Hong Kong Chinese do not regard those from Vietnam as fellow countrymen. Remarks such as "they are coarse and unruly" or "they have adopted Vietnamese habits" are common amongst Chinese restauranteurs. At the same time, a number of Hong Kong restaurant and take-away owners offered jobs to the new arrivals from Vietnam. In most cases, however, these were menial jobs in the kitchen, such as washing-up or as kitchen assistants.

9

We Are Here to Stay: From Sojourner to Settler

The Chinese have been regarded as a self-reliant community who, by and large, help themselves and sort out their own problems. As we have already seen, the pattern of migration based on kinship and village networks did smooth the passage for arriving male workers who were found work within a self-contained sector, the Chinese catering trade. Again, the Chinese cultural tradition, which stressed respect and obedience towards authority, made it more acceptable for overseas Chinese to tackle their problems by themselves. The lack of a democratic tradition in Hong Kong also served to confine Chinese ambitions and aspirations to the economic sector, namely to acquiring material wealth.

With the arrival of wives, children and elderly dependants from Hong Kong, the Chinese community in Britain had to cope with a host of new problems, as their children had to be educated, larger accommodation had to be found for their families, and family members had to be confident enough to go shopping and use the public transport system.

Evidence suggests that the Chinese are having a hard time coming to terms with their new life in Britain. Incidents of racial hostility and discrimination have not helped matters. As the Chinese became a more settled community, the authorities finally realized that the Chinese also suffer from the same lack of opportunities and disadvantages as other ethnic groups in Britain. In 1983, therefore, a Parliamentary Inquiry (Race Relations and Immigration Sub-Committee), was set up to examine the problems and needs of the Chinese community.

Education for a Better Life

In the old China, learning was valued as a means of self-cultivation. It also enabled the successful to aspire to prestigious careers as scholars and government officials. Esteem towards the educated is still very much an aspect of Chinese culture today.

The value placed on education can be clearly seen in the Chow family. All four sons are well-educated. James Chow, Shing Tung's brother, recently took one year off from running the family restaurant in Enfield, to study for an M.A. degree at the London School of Oriental and African Studies. The Chows have always had a scholarly background. Shing Tung's father was educated at a private school in Peking and his brothers went to university in China before the Communist revolution. However, even the Chinese from the New Territories, Hong Kong, place importance on their children's education. David Wan has just graduated with a degree in Electrical Engineering from Thames Polytechnic. He would like to take a further degree in Business Studies, but realizes that he would have to work for a few years first. In general, the overseas Chinese take a pragmatic view of education, in terms of its subsequent earning-potential. This would account for the popularity of professions such as law, accountancy, medicine and engineering. Whilst valuing their children's education, however, many Chinese who run take-aways still expect their children to help out in the business, as often the demands of the family enterprise are seen as more important than the career ambitions of children.

Generally speaking, the wealthier restauranteurs and professional families prefer to send their children to public school. As we shall see, this is largely a reaction to the perceived lack of discipline and "non-academic" climate in the state schools. Alfred Chan, however, opposes the concept of private school. He felt that the state schools provided a good learning environment not only academically, but also in preparing for adulthood. Alfred, therefore, thought his son, Kwan Yu, would benefit from coping with some of the "rougher" kids in comprehensive schools.

The situation of latecomers to the British educational system is particularly disturbing. Chinese youngsters who have spent only two to three years in British secondary schools are not only educationally disadvantaged, but also more likely to have problems adjusting to life in Britain. Kenneth Wan, David's brother, spent only one year in a British secondary school. Like David, he subsequently went to a further education college to sit for his "O" levels. David Wan could not understand a word of what his teacher said when he first arrived. His first few months were spent at the language centre on an intensive language learning course. In order to keep up with the lessons, David would in his first year simply copy his teachers' notes or passages from the textbooks.

Different cultural expectations of the teacher's role in school also cause great strains on the new arrival. Learning, for the Chinese, simply means studying from books. This contrasts sharply with the expressionistic approach in British schools. Not surprisingly, therefore, many Chinese parents regard much of the school activities as irrelevant. Chinese parents have also complained about the lack of discipline in British schools, for, in Hong Kong, discipline is strict, with the authority of the teacher seen as an extension of that of the family head. Chinese children entering British schools at the age of 13-15 years are particularly affected by the sudden change. Most of these new arrivals would not have seen their parents for many years. Others would have been sent back to Hong Kong for several years before rejoining their parents in Britain when in their teens.

Alfred Chan and Shing Tung Chow do not have any kind words for Hong Kong's educational system. The early schools owed their growth to wealthy businessmen and religious charities. Since 1974, the Hong Kong government has introduced free primary and junior secondary education, covering nine years in all. It is openly recognized that most schools are under-resourced and that teachers, particularly those teaching English language, are badly-trained. David Wan recalled his primary school in the town of Sha Tin. The school had 1,000 pupils, classrooms were overcrowded and there had to be a morning and an afternoon shift. Generally speaking, the "brighter" pupils attended morning school.

Recently, educationists have begun to question the use of English as the main medium of instruction in most secondary schools. Hong Kong is largely a mono-lingual society, with most people speaking Cantonese. Yet, at the end of three years' secondary education, many Chinese pupils are only semi-literate in both Chinese and English. Poorly-trained teachers and outdated teaching methods result in Chinese pupils acquiring, at best, a "book knowledge" of English. At the same time, with the emphasis on English in secondary school, many Chinese children are unable to write Chinese fluently.

For many Chinese parents, Hong Kong schools are doing their job, because of the amount of homework given to their children. According to David Wan, "In Hong Kong, it is strictly compulsory. Often you would get punished by having to explain in front of the whole class why your homework was not done." The emphasis on homework has created a scramble amongst schoolchildren for quiet places to study. Because of overcrowded conditions at home, many children would be found studying in public parks and even in Kaitak airport's passenger terminal lounge.

The Catering Boom Goes Into Reverse

There have been indications in recent years that the growth in the Chinese restaurant trade has slowed down tremendously and in some places there has even been a fall in the number of restaurants. The economic recession and the higher VAT rates introduced several years ago have certainly adversely affected business in restaurants outside Soho Chinatown. Business has declined by over 100 per cent in the last five years of the Chow family's restaurant in Enfield.

In Edinburgh, the restaurant trade is seasonal. According to Alfred Chan, Chinese restaurants in Edinburgh would lay off chefs and waiters during the winter months, so as to cut their overheads. With the recession, some of these workers are being laid off permanently. Without alternative skills and lacking fluency in English, these workers are unlikely to find new employment.

Ironically, the reluctance of many young second-generation Chinese to work in restaurants has created a severe shortage of labour in some Chinese eating establishments. The considerable reduction in work permits issued for catering work – fewer than 100 issued per year – has also contributed to this shortage. Because of it, a number of non-Chinese waiters have been employed not only in suburban Chinese restaurants but also in the heart of Liverpool's Chinatown.

English: A Language for Survival

Not surprisingly, lack of fluency in English affects not only the school work of Chinese children, but also their future job prospects. For many Chinese teenagers coming to Britain at the age of 13 or 14, their first encounter with English would have been at secondary school either in Hong Kong or in Britain. Most Chinese parents in the restaurant trade speak some form of Chinese to their children at home.

It is not uncommon to find restaurant workers speaking either no English whatsoever or only a few stock phrases of English, despite having been in the country for 20 years or longer. Kitchen staff are particularly isolated and so have no opportunity to speak English at all. In recent years, some Chinese restaurants have been staffed by young workers from urban Hong Kong who are not only more conversant in English, but also have a higher standard of English. Elderly mothers are also unlikely to speak any English. Shing Tung's mother, Lee Man Wun, whose native tongue is Mandarin, speaks only a few words of English. His grandmother, who is 82, speaks no English at all.

As mentioned already, the long, unsocial hours worked and the lack of intensive language instruction facilities at convenient times have contributed to this situation. Some Chinese educationists feel that the existing language instruction is not sensitive to the language difficulties of Chinese adults mainly from rural backgrounds. In September 1983 the Chinese Chamber of Commerce set up English language classes for members of the Chinese community, in co-operation with the Inner London Education Authority. The classes are held daily from Monday to Friday at the Chamber of Commerce's Chinese School in Frith Street, Soho.

Restaurant workers and their families can attend all the sessions or just one class a week, according to their work commitments.

It should be noted that the totally different grammatical structure and script used in Chinese do present severe difficulties for Chinese speakers learning English. Whereas written English is based on a Romanic alphabet, the Chinese script is ideographic, involving the use of simple and complex characters. Each character is mono-syllabic, whereas most English words have more than one syllable.

The Hopes and Frustrations of our Younger Generation

Chinese social workers have in recent years dealt with a number of cases involving school-leavers and teenagers "lost to the system" and to their family. In several cases, they became easy "fodder" for recruitment into the Triads. The lack of suitable vocational training and further education opportunities has denied these adolescents a second chance. Particularly vulnerable are those children who joined their parents in Britain in their teens. Lacking confidence and leaving school with no qualifications, many of these youngsters enter catering work as a last resort.

Unlike their parents, many of the young second-generation Chinese who were either born in Britain or joined their parents here at a later age have set their sights on careers outside catering. Some working-class youngsters, of course, would like to become "top waiters" in a Chinese restaurant, just as some of the children of wealthy restaurant owners would, one day, like to run their own restaurant. Outside catering, many Chinese teenagers from working-class backgrounds would like to be fitters, electricians or even football stars. The lucky ones do succeed. In January 1977, the 15-year-old son of Mr Pang, a restaurant owner in Amersham, was signed on by Southampton football club. Chinese girls not resigned to a life of housework and home sewing are attracted to office jobs such as a bank clerk or to jobs in the caring professions such as nursing. Not surprisingly, middle-class Chinese children tend to have higher expectations.

Alfred Chan, who is conducting research into the employment needs of Chinese youngsters, has come across a number of Chinese teenagers suffering frustration and alienation. Teenage delinquency has taken the form of truancy from school, shop-lifting, carrying offensive weapons and even glue-sniffing. Some of these teenagers only recently arrived in Britain and had not seen their parents for 8-10 years. The usual teenage problems of growing up are heightened in many ways for these teenagers.

The parents of these alienated teenagers usually would have had only a basic education in Hong Kong. Alfred knew of several families who, because they were too busy earning a living, could offer little comfort to their children. In some cases, the fathers refused to accept responsibility for their sons' deviant behaviour. Typically, they would in Confucian fashion say that their sons "have gone astray". Alfred thought that the Chinese concern for reputation and "saving face" was counter-productive. In his own words, "Under the banner of family disgrace and community reputation we try to 'cover the fire with dry paper'. But we simply can't ignore the problem away."

The picture is not one of total gloom, however. Chinese children from catering backgrounds, even the late arrivals, have succeeded in entering the professions and obtaining higher qualifications. David Wan is an example.

It would also be untrue to say that all Chinese teenagers have conflicts with their parents. In fact, it is still quite common for a son to take over his parents' take-away or restaurant when they retire. Even a number of those who have entered the professions would later leave their job, in order to run the family business and care for their elderly parents. So, filial duty does not always have to be forced on a child. Alfred told me about a girl attending a further education course in Edinburgh. She came to Britain four years ago and is still very Chinese in many respects. She would always stay at home to accompany her mother and help with the cooking. Her English friends, however, would often be out at night or at the local youth club.

We Are Only Human

The tendency of Chinese families to keep their problems to themselves may give the impression that the Chinese are totally capable of caring for themselves. But the Chinese also have their share of marital breakdowns, unemployment, family breakdowns and social isolation.

Language and cultural barriers often mean a lifetime of loneliness for those elderly women and young wives not directly involved in catering work. Often, these women are left to cope by themselves with their children's upbringing. For the elderly, a lifetime of hard work in the restaurants has left many Chinese workers with severe health problems, often requiring them to retire prematurely. In some cases, the elderly men have no families to look after them, because their children either are all out at work or do not wish to care for their fathers.

In Liverpool's Chinatown area, there are two houses that provide accommodation for the elderly. Although the conditions are spartan and the premises fairly run-down, the adjacent Chinese shops and restaurants provide a sense of community for the elderly lodgers. Chinese community workers in Camden recently set up a Chinese Women's Group for elderly women and divorcees living alone. They meet once a week and take part in a range of activities such as keep-fit classes, watching educational films, sewing or just having a general chat. The popularity of these activities can be seen from the fact that some of the women come all the way from Lewisham to attend the central London meetings. Camden's Chinese also have a Men's Group catering for the needs of unemployed and elderly Chinese from both Hong Kong and Vietnam. A number of the unemployed men were restaurant chefs and waiters

Elderly members of Camden Chinese Women's Group at their weekly meeting held at the YWCA in central London. One or two of the women come from as far as Lewisham to attend these sessions.

who had either been made redundant or had retired early, because of physical disabilities.

Broken homes and split families are not uncommon in the Chinese community. Despite the Chinese emphasis on filial duty, grandparents may sometimes be deserted by their children. There also have been cases of husbands running away with another woman, leaving the wife to care for the children. Wives have also left their husbands because of their gambling habits. More tragic examples include mothers who died in psychiatric care or who committed suicide because either their children or husband had deserted them. The normal reaction to all this would be to suggest that these elderly Chinese be taken into care or placed in a home. However, in 1981 Mrs Lim Shu Pao, Camden's Chinese community worker, felt strongly against this. "To suggest to an elderly Chinese person to go to a day centre or old people's home would be like sending them to the moon" (*Solving the Chinese Puzzle*, 1981).

According to Mrs Lim, the elderly should be able to live in the way to which they are accustomed, which is basically as part of an extended family. The growing number of broken families and the plight of the single elderly are tackled by an exciting new idea of Mrs Lim – the "mini-commune". As an experiment in shelter housing, the "mini-commune" would provide a home for the disabled, the elderly, single-parent families and children in care. This would enable the elderly to live in familiar surroundings as part of an extended family and create for the children an environment suffused with their culture and traditions. Commune members would not be bound by blood ties or marriage but by genuine friendship and respect. Such a group would be, at least, partially self-supporting with income derived from vegetable-gardening and poultry-rearing.

The awareness of these social problems has encouraged the growth of new community organizations to improve the socio-economic status of the Chinese in Britain. These organizations, such as Camden Chinese Community Centre and Merseyside Chinese Community Service, assume from the start that the Chinese are a permanent community in Britain. In their contacts with the Chinese, they seek to convince them that there is no "loss of face" in claiming welfare benefits or applying for council housing. Merseyside Chinese Community Service moved into its new premises in 1982 in the impressive "Pagoda of Hundred Harmony", built with the help of a £250,000 Urban-Aid grant. The Centre provides a range of advisory

The "Pagoda of Hundred Harmony", Liverpool's new Chinese community centre, built at a cost of £250,000.

Brian Wang demonstrating a movement of *Tai Chi Chuan*, an ancient form of spiritual and physical exercise. In the background a Chinese poem inscribed by Mr Wang on the front wall of the new Chinese community centre in Liverpool.

and interpretation services to the Liverpool Chinese. It also has a nursery run by volunteers and provides a range of leisure activities such as table-tennis for youngsters. Brian Wang, the Taiwan-born Chinese co-ordinator, also broadcasts a weekly news programme in Chinese on Radio Merseyside.

We Are Here To Stay

By now, it should be clear that the Chinese have, by and large, become a settled community in Britain. The arrival of the migrants' families from Hong Kong and the uncertainty over the territory's future have no doubt influenced the move towards settlement. It is true, of course, that some of the New Territories migrants still consciously think of returning to their home villages to retire. Yet, at the same time, they have acquired a degree of permanence in Britain by having bought a house here and even having children or grandchildren born in this country. Such contradictions do occur, because old ways of thinking often take a lifetime to be superseded. One reason why some restaurant workers still harbour the aim of returning home is that they feel a need to be recognized and respected for their achievements. The Chinese have always been conscious of the need to openly display the signs of material or academic success, so as to enhance the status of their families within the community. So, according to the Chinese saying, a migrant is "walking about at night in embroidered robes" if he acquires wealth in a foreign land without visibly demonstrating the fruits of this success to his "own people" back home.

The 1982 Nationality Act has also convinced many Chinese of the need to remain in Britain and call for their families to join them if they have not done so already. Assuming that China regains sovereignty over Hong Kong in the near future, those Hong Kong Chinese holding British passports would in effect be stateless if they did not opt for Chinese citizenship.

Let us now return to our three families to see what their plans are regarding settlement. Shing Tung Chow thought that most Chinese were here to stay, irrespective of what they might say. Although Shing Tung's mother still lacks confidence in Britain, she is unlikely to return to Hong Kong as, in her son's words, "She has nothing to go back to". Shing Tung himself would only consider returning to Hong

Kong if there were reforms in the political system in the direction of greater democracy.

On the surface, it would seem that the Wan family are planning to retire in Hong Kong. With their savings they have bought two houses in Sha Tin and Tai Wai in the New Territories. Mrs Wan still misses Hong Kong with its Chinese cultural environment and way of life. Yet David Wan thought his parents were unlikely to return home because of uncertainty over Hong Kong's future. David himself likes living in Britain. "After coming to Britain for 20 years, when you try to go back to Hong Kong to work you couldn't. Like my father, he could go back to Hong Kong but he wouldn't get a job."

Alfred and Alice Chan would like to stay in Britain, particularly because of the educational opportunities open to their son, Kwan Yu. Although the first two years in Britain were both financially and emotionally hard for the Chans, Alfred and Alice are now both happy with their new environment in Scotland. The Chans thought, however, that they could re-adjust to life in Hong Kong if necessary, although they would miss the better and more spacious accommodation in Britain. Furthermore, according to Alfred "Class differences here are not so glaring compared with Hong Kong. In Hong Kong, if you're rich, you dress to kill as people tend to judge you on what you wear".

Master Jimmy Chan coaching martial arts students of Hung Gar Kung Fu School in Liverpool. Kung fu is becoming popular with young people of all races.

A Visible Community

Until recently, the Chinese in Britain have kept a "low profile" and were not known for asserting their rights in their adopted country. Today, with more and more Chinese in occupations other than catering and with the presence of Chinese families in housing estates and Chinese children in British schools, they have become targets of resentment, just as the early Chinese seamen who were seen as a threat by the indigenous working-class.

The Chinese are as vulnerable to racial discrimination as any other visible ethnic group in Britain. In 1982 white shopkeepers in Birmingham tried to prevent the City Council from granting planning permission to Chinese who wanted to open a bookshop in St Martin's House Parade (Birmingham Bullring). Alfred Chan, in his work, has come across numerous cases involving Chinese being harassed or discriminated against. Chinese children are bullied at school and the walls of their families' council flats are daubed with racist slogans. Alice Chan recalled that when she was working in the East End as a hospital nurse, some of the white patients refused to be touched by Chinese and other Asian nurses.

Chinese children probably suffer more from "name teasing" than any other ethnic group. Many teachers see Chinese children as vulnerable because they do not assert themselves in the classroom or playground. We have already seen that the strict Confucian upbringing in Chinese homes stresses obedience and the control of one's emotions. Shing Tung Chow thought, however, that the *"kung-fu"* image of the Chinese, popularized through the films of Bruce Lee, has done a world of good in making people think that the Chinese are all experts in the martial arts.

David Wan was constantly teased about his "funny" name at school, but he did not take this seriously. More serious, however, is the racial abuse suffered by Chinese restauranteurs. David remembered one night when an English customer entered his parents' take-away and said, "You took all our wealth from us. This is our country. You just come here to take all of our things away". After ordering his chips he left peacefully. Fights between unruly white customers and members of the Chow family in their Enfield restaurant are a frequent occurrence. Shing Tung said that the Chinese are very vulnerable to "eat and run" customers who think they can "pull the wool" over the Chinese waiters' eyes. After eating most of the meal the customer would refuse to pay the bill, arguing that the food was "bad" or not up to standard. Yet a few weeks later that customer would return with the intention of trying the same trick again.

To some extent, China's emergence as a world power has instilled a sense of pride and confidence in Britain's Chinese and increased their standing as a minority group here. At least, this was the view of Charles Cheung, a Christian pastor and restauranteur in Liverpool. "Overseas Chinese have this feeling that because their mother country is stronger, they are somebody. It's a psychological difference when you walk in the street. There's a little bit less jeering and talking behind our backs. People are more interested to talk about China, and when they look at you and speak to you, they have a certain kind of respect" (*Daily Telegraph*, 2 January 1977).

Integration is Not a One-Way Process

Until the last decade or so, integration in society has been regarded as a simple one-way process involving the new immigrant gradually assimilating the values and life-style of the host population. A mastery of English was, therefore, seen as the first thing that an immigrant should acquire in order to feel accepted in Britain. As long as the immigrant did not learn English, therefore, he deserved to be discriminated against and looked down upon. This notion of integration is still prevalent today in many British institutions. Alfred recently told me of a case involving a 12-year old Chinese girl, born in Britain, who was too ashamed to invite her parents to any school functions because they spoke little or no English.

At least some institutions today have begun to accept the argument that a genuinely multi-racial society should not only tolerate but actively encourage cultural diversity. The Chinese in Britain do not only share certain common experiences with white British citizens; they also have a distinctive cultural identity. Furthermore, the growing influence of certain aspects of Chinese culture in Britain can only enrich the existing traditions in this country. The mother-tongue issue is of great importance to the Chinese in Britain. Alfred Chan in

Edinburgh is actively trying to unite the efforts of the three Chinese part-time language classes in the city. David Wan said that he would make sure that his children would one day be able to at least speak (if not write) Chinese. Alfred Chan would like his son, Kwan Yu, to maintain his cultural identity whilst at the same time being integrated with the local white children.

A growing number of young Chinese professionals, like Alfred Chan, feel, however, that the Chinese have to discard those cultural elements or traditions which are inappropriate or a barrier to participating in a modern society. Traditional values should be respected but they can also be a barrier to integration. According to Alfred, "It is sheer hypocrisy to stress the virtues of family loyalty and obedience on the one hand whilst at the same time exploiting family ties by, for example, employing nephews and cousins for a pittance under the pretext of helping them out". Other Chinese community workers have stressed the need to open channels of communication with the host community, to acquire full rights as citizens.

Many young second-generation Chinese face an identity crisis. The Liverpool-born actor, David Yip, star of the BBC TV series *The Chinese Detective*, once referred to the "grey area" of British society in which children of mixed-parentage lived, neither white nor black. Having a Chinese father and English mother, David Yip is only just discovering his Chinese roots. In his own words, "My Chinese cultural background is a newly-acquired one, and I am still acquiring it". Yet, in the world of television and advertising, the Chinese are portrayed in ways which do not reflect the changing reality of their situation in Britain. In order to pander to the most debased sense of humour, the Chinese appear in the most derogatory stereotyped roles, as "goon-like" chefs or waiters, sloganizing "Maoists" or inscrutable "Fu Manchu-like" gangsters.

The Chinese presence in Britain has not only contributed to the catering economy. A civilization as old and well-developed as the Chinese can only enrich the existing traditions of the host society. The growing acceptance and popularity of martial arts, *Tai Chi Chuan* and traditional Chinese medicine in the West are examples of the positive contributions of the Chinese overseas. *Tai Chi Chuan* is an age-old system of mental and physical exercise designed to promote good health and enhance the practitioner's defence capabilities. It is based on a system of rythmic movements and postures which increases physical awareness and improves the body's general circulation.

Perhaps the best example of cultural enrichment in a multi-racial society can be found in the activities of Brian Wang's Tai-Shen Chinese Play Association in Liverpool. Not only is the association concerned to preserve and nurture Chinese traditional dance, theatre and acrobatics in Britain, it has also recruited a team of whites, Eurasians and Chinese as performing artists. In some of the performances, English dockworkers, plumbers and even an MP have performed side by side with Chinese restaurant workers. Liverpool also has a multi-racial traditional Chinese orchestra which provides the music for many of the Chinese opera and dance productions.

Whether this form of integration based on harmony and mutual respect will be allowed to blossom, only time will tell. One thing for sure, the Chinese are unlikely to accept being assimilated in a straightforward manner in this country.

Book List

N. Fitchett, *Chinese Children in Derby*, Jan. 1976 (published as a pamphlet as part of a diploma course)

Fung Yulan, *History of Chinese Philosophy*, (ed. Derk Bodde), The Free Press, 1966

Ann Garvey and Brian Jackson, *Chinese Children*, National Educational Research and Development Trust, 1975

Hong Kong Research Project, *Hong Kong: A Case To Answer*, Spokesman Books, 1974

D. Howard Smith, *Confucius*, Paladin Books (Grenada Publ. Ltd), 1974

D. Jones, *The Chinese in Britain: Origins and Development of a Community*, New Community Vol VII No.13, 1979

Lim Shu Pao, *Solving the Chinese Puzzle*, Community Care Jan. 8th, 1981

Irene Loh Lynn, *The Chinese Community in Liverpool*, Merseyside Area Profile Group, 1982

Stanford M. Lyman, *Chinese America*, New York, 1974

J.P. May, *The Chinese in Britain: 1860-1914*, in C. Holmes (ed.) "Immigrants and Minorities in British Society", George Allen & Unwin, 1978

H. Brett Melandry, *The Oriental Americans*, Ta Wyne Publishing Inc., 1972

Ng Kwee Choo, *The Chinese in London*, Institute of Race Relations, OUP, 1968

Sean O'Callaghan, *The Triads: The Mafia of the Far East*, W.H. Allen & Co, 1981

J. Watson, *Emigration and the Chinese Lineage*, University of California Press, 1975

J. Watson, *Restaurants and Remittances: Chinese Emigrant Workers in London*, in G.M. Foster and R.V. Kemper "Anthropologists in Cities", Little Brown & Co., Boston, 1974

Leslie Wong, *Overseas Chinese in Britain Yearbook*, Overseas Chinese Service, London, 1972

Picture Acknowledgments

The Author and Publishers would like to thank the following for their kind permission to use copyright pictures in the book: Klaus Barisch, page 35; BBC Hulton Picture Library, pages 5 (bottom), 9, 16; Alfred and Alice Chan, page 42; C.K. Chan, pages 18 (top), 57 (bottom), 58; Federal Publications (S) Pte Ltd, page 51 (from *Fun with Chinese Characters Vol I*); Government Information Services, Hong Kong, page 40 (bottom); Sally and Richard Greenhill, pages 18 (bottom), 19, 40 (top), 57 (top); Hong Kong Government Office, pages 17, 54; The Save the Children Fund, page 59 (Camilla Jessel). The drawings on page 47 are from *Animals of the Chinese Zodiac* by T.C. Lai (Hong Kong Book Centre). The map on page 15 was drawn by R.F. Brien. All other pictures in the book are copyright of Anthony Shang.

Cover pictures

The colour picture on the front cover shows Chinese New Year (The Metropolitan Police Public Information Department). The background picture shows London's Chinatown, April 1911 (BBC Hulton Picture Library). The black and white photograph shows one of the partners of Fung Shing restaurant in Soho cutting up a roast duck, Cantonese-style (Anthony Shang).

Index